hook, line and thinker

ANGLING & ETHICS

Alexander Schwab

First published by Merlin Unwin Books, Ludlow, in 2003
Merlin Unwin Books
Palmers House
7 Corve Street
Ludlow
Shropshire SY8 1DB   U.K.

ISBN 1 873674 59 7
Typeset by Think Graphic Design, Ludlow, UK.
Printed and bound in Great Britain by Biddles Ltd, Guildford.

Also published by Merlin Unwin Books

Email: books@merlinunwin.co.uk
Website: www.countrybooksdirect.com

Confessions of a Shooting Fishing Man
Laurence Catlow

A History of Flyfishing
Conrad Voss Bark

Going Fishing
Negley Farson

The Far from Compleat Angler
Tom Fort

Fishing up the Moon
Harry Parsons

hook, line and thinker

ANGLING & ETHICS

MERLIN
UNWIN
·BOOKS·

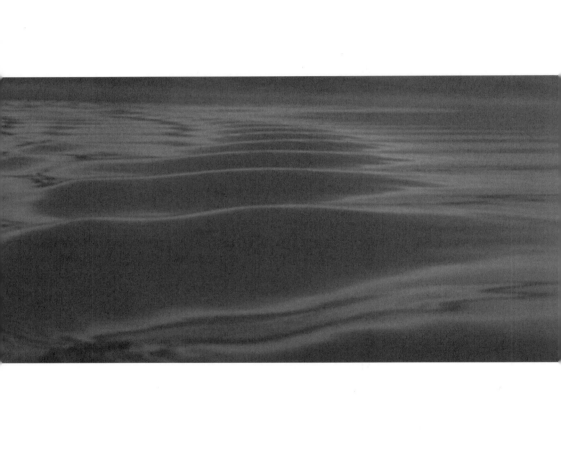

Contents

Preface and acknowledgements

Fishermen are by definition optimists – they go fishing with a spring in their step assuming they're in with a sporting chance of catching a fish. Fishermen are also given to telling stories and to thinking about God and the world. A rich literature over centuries testifies to the great tradition of recreational angling.

In recent decades, however, a storm has been brewing. Part of public opinion no longer sees fishing as a harmless, tranquil pastime but rather as an abuse of nature and the torture of fish. At the core of this radical change of attitude is the idea of animal rights and all it entails. The animal rights movement has gathered such momentum and influence that it has the ear of governmental circles all over Europe and the United States. Siding with "suffering" animals, preferably of the cuddly variety, is a sure vote winner in market-orientated politics. What the real issues are gets completely blurred and I doubt if all animal rights supporters and sympathisers actually fully understand what they are supporting. Animal welfare ideas such as the prevention of cruelty to animals are a world apart from animal rights ideas granting apes, dogs, rats and cockroaches the same moral and eventually legal rights as human beings. It doesn't stop there. Infanticide, for example, is argued by some animal rights supporters to be permissible, whereas eating shrimps or going fishing are wrong.

Animal rights philosophies are the foundation of anti-angling, anti-hunting and anti-country life. Farming, horse riding, mushroom stalking – you name it; under the sceptre of animal rights philosophies, practically any present day country business or pleasure pursuit is out of the question. No compromise – the mercilessness towards its opponents is one of the hallmarks of a movement which sails under the flag of compassion. Quite often animal rights and extreme environmentalism go hand in hand. Fundamental environmentalism is the idea that man is a blot on earthscape – an unfortunate evolutionary aberration. The idea was perfectly expressed by a demonstrator sporting a banner saying: "Save the planet, kill yourself!"

Animal rights and fundamental environmentalism can't be dismissed as the crackpot ideas of a few university professors. The seductive power of these ideas has permeated far too deeply into the fabric of teaching and politics on all levels. It has done so over the years by remorselessly hammering home the message that Christianity and Western culture are the root of all evil in the human and animal world. Pulling the rug from under Christianity and Western culture is a high priority in the animal rights agenda. Animal rights is the lever for a fundamental change in morals and society.

By explaining and exposing what animal rights is really all about, I hope to contribute to the opinion which no longer accepts the mindless propaganda of animal rights. Animal welfare must not be confused with animal rights. Animal rights should be opposed on all levels whereas many if not most animal welfare projects deserve support. Anti-fishing and anti-hunting are no longer the key issues – the nub relates to the dissolution of the web of values that sustain us. The fight for fishing, hunting and country life in general is about fundamental values. Regardless of your religious or political beliefs, as a fisherman and hunter the challenge is to think clearly and to stem the rising tide. Like you I want to go on fishing, hunting and mushroom stalking. This is why this book was written.

Some source material is only available on the Internet. The URLs are operational at the time of writing. URLs change or sites are taken off the Net. Anybody interested in a specific source and not able to look it up can contact me at www.philosofish.ch – I'll be happy to supply a copy of the print-out. Many people have in one way or another contributed to *Hook, Line and Thinker* which, of course, doesn't mean that they share my views. Despite the generous assistance and advice I have received, there might still be errors in the book for which I fully and unconditionally accept responsibility.

Roland Henrion, my Belgian fishing friend currently working as a fishing guide in the Seychelles, opened new fishing horizons for me. He is the most 'compleat' angler I have ever met. Some of his remarks in the relaxed atmosphere at the bar on Desroches Island have set me on the right track. There is another important Roland: Roland Wüthrich, with whom I share a boat on Switzerland's most beautiful water, Lake Thun. I have learned a lot from Roland about fishing and mushroom stalking. Roland is a master mushroom stalker. Dr. Peter Fraser, Senior Lecturer in Zoology at the University of Aberdeen, was very generous and helpful. Dr. Bernhard Streb kept me up-to-date with scientific background information and Kate Sanderson, special adviser to the Faroese Prime Minister's Office, offered valuable critical remarks and suggestions.

A special thank-you goes to distant San Diego, to Richard Louv author of *Fly-fishing for Sharks*. Richard was the first to read the draft and his words of encouragement were not just reassuring but highly motivating. Thanks Richard! Dr. David Oderberg, presently Reader in Philosophy at the University of Reading, has helped me to avoid pitfalls on the philosophical side. His feedback was incisive, challenging, stimulating and greatly appreciated! Many thanks also to the editors Karen and Merlin Unwin for taking *Hook, Line and Thinker* on board and their hospitality and generosity. The fisherman's wife's lot is not always an easy one. Over the years my wife Regina has carried the burden with saintly patience and tolerance. There are compensations: such as fresh trout; or this book, which is dedicated to Regina.

Biglen, Switzerland
6.10.2002

Links, background and lots more at

www.philosofish.ch

Introduction

Inside the washing machine

*"*Killer, killer!" Anxiously I looked behind me. Nobody there. The scene was positively bizarre. There I was on my own outside the trade fair hall. Improbable as it may seem there was actually nobody to be seen leaving at the same time as me. And by coincidence there were no visitors approaching. "Killer, killer!" Facing me was a crowd of about fifty angry animal rights activists. Their vociferousness and the threatening gestures intensified to frenzy level as I walked towards them. I did so confidently, not because I am particularly courageous but because of a dozen police officers between me and the delirious protesters.

What exactly were these people trying to tell me and my fellow fishermen and hunters (it was a fishing and hunting fair) with "killer" and other assorted abuse? The basic message seemed to be that fishing and hunting are criminal activities akin to murder. I say "seemed" because this wasn't the occasion for an exchange of views or even a discussion. Such incidents could be shrugged off were it not for the fact that there is a growing internationally influential movement with "animal rights" and "animal liberation" on its banners, a movement which poses a potential threat to fishing. Any argument about man and animals sooner or later also homes in on the angler. The bottom line will inevitably involve a variant of this theme:

> *The very real challenge to anglers, then, is to find a justification for their cruel treatment of animals (fish), a justification which must also satisfy the ethical hunter's requirement for the humane treatment of animals (game). Unless such justification is found, I see no clear resolution of this dilemma other than for hunters and society generally to abandon all sport fishing.*[1]

This is the academically and politically correct way to tell you that you're a moral scandal. The reason no fisherman should ignore the issues thus raised is quite simply that if the field is left to the anti-anglers, that is, to

---

1 A. Dionys de Leeuw, *Environmental Ethics*, "Contemplating the Interests of Fish: The Angler's Challenge", Winter 1996, Vol.18, No.4, pp.373-390. (http://www.cep.unt.edu/staff.html)

animal rights activists, your fishing might be gone sooner than you think. Part of the challenge is to understand what is argued by the opponents of fishing.

Philosophy in the scholarly sense isn't everybody's idea of fun. Yet at the bottom of all militant and latent anti-angling is philosophy – in both the popular and the scholarly sense of the word. Philosophy in the popular sense has something to do with wisdom, with what the world is like, with what one actually should or should not do. Practical philosophy as it were. Philosophy in the scholarly sense is an academic study concerned with the systematic examination of concepts such as ethics, causality and freedom. One doesn't exclude the other. Both meanings of philosophy are of importance to the fisherman, because scholarly philosophy in one way or another translates into practical philosophy. Philosophers do take sides, recommend this, that or the other. If fishing is going to be banned, restricted or otherwise meddled with it will be on philosophical grounds. In *Hook, Line and Thinker* the most important of these views are explored and critically scrutinised. In plain English. As plain as possible, anyway.

My second goal is to present reflections and arguments which answer the fundamental charges against fishing. And what hopefully emerges out of it all is a piece of practical help for the fisherman: at least some landmarks and useful suggestions for his thinking on fishing. Some of the arguments I present look fairly conclusive to me – but what answers a question for one man raises a problem for the next. All philosophers profess to follow logic and most do. Yet they arrive at wildly differing conclusions. Logic is rarely at fault. It is more often than not the premises and the interpretation of the facts which give arguments some surprising turns. Like in real life:

Fishing the flats is one of the most exciting and beautiful piscatorial experiences. I was introduced to fishing the flats in the Seychelles by Roland Henrion – the best all-round angler I have ever met. The wonderworld of the flats can be treacherous. You need to be taught about its dangers. Stepping on an almost perfectly camouflaged ray is an adventure you can do without. You don't simply stomp out there and start flogging the sea! Anyway, there I was on my first solo flight, so to speak. No Roland to supervise and explain what was happening. Just me. I had studied the tidal table, I had the right equipment, I was confident and knew the place I had chosen for my solo. The reef there runs just over half a mile from the shore. Between the shore and the flats there is a channel washed out by tidal currents about 100 yards wide and at its deepest maybe six to ten feet deep. At low tide you hardly notice the depth of the channel because it rises and falls so gently.

So it's off for the reef, the incoming tide and the action. Looking back shoreward, I see the lush green hills silhouetted against a sky so intensely blue that it would humble any postcard. A small cotton-wool cloud hovers decoratively in the blue infinity. The gentle wind carries birdsong and the mysterious perfume of the tropical forest. I encounter the first ray which glides in slow motion through the water – there is unsurpassed grace and elegance in its movement. It provokes a distinct thumping in the heart region but after another two rays fly gently past I sort of merge with the situation and shuffle confidently about. The fishing completely absorbs me. I hook an emperor, a few snappers and spot what I think is a barracuda. I fish for it but it doesn't show interest. The tide rises and it's time to head for terra firma.

Easier said than done. In all my dreamlike moving about, drinking in the fishing and surrounding beauty, I hadn't noticed that the wind had picked up considerably. Or I may have noticed but the message didn't register in the right quarters, perhaps because the wind helped my casting. Bad fishing if you think about it. Very bad. The pretty little cloud was now looking distinctly menacing as it rapidly descended on me. Before I knew what was happening I found myself in the middle of it. Visibility zero and the water whipping up around me. The temperature dropping sharply – to chilly. The rain pouring and the humidity were such that I was afraid of drowning by breathing too deeply. This must be what it feels like inside a washing machine. I wasn't really scared, more stunned or shocked – or maybe I just prefer to think that I wasn't scared.

Anyway, by the time that mobile piece of landscape was through with me, the tide had considerably risen and I was still way out. Swimming that channel would be inevitable. I wondered vaguely if there was a current which would drag me right back out. When I reached the channel I arranged my bag and gear so that I wouldn't lose half of it and then I started swimming. A one-handed breast stroke, for in the other hand I held the rod. After about twenty yards the lure, a liberal interpretation of a Clauser Minnow, came unstuck from the cork handle where I had fixed it. A fad of mine given up since. You can see it coming now, can't you? The Clauser dangled so enticingly behind me that this colossal garfish couldn't resist and took. Swimming I might have been but my fisherman's instincts didn't fail me: I clung firmly onto the rod with the result that the leviathan pulled me right back to where I'd come from. There I quite literally dug my heels in and got down to business. And what a business it was! The giant was well hooked and a struggle of epic dimensions ensued while the tide, unimpressed by the event, steadily rose. Finally, the water well up to my neck, and I was eye to eye with my fate, so to speak. And this is where all anglers will find themselves, if they refuse to address the big issues. By the way, the fish weighed 20lbs at the very least.

I take liberties of style. This adds a touch of lightness to what can often seem an obscure subject and a bore for those who aren't keen on philosophical discourse. But why should ethics in general and those of fishing in particular be the exclusive domain of so-called experts? After all, it's the non-experts who bear the brunt of philosophical action. *Hook, Line and Thinker* is for those interested in the issues involved, especially anglers and hunters. The wisdom of this undertaking might be questioned by some fellow anglers on the grounds that, by taking anti-anglers seriously, one actually helps their cause by giving it publicity. There are two important points here.

The first one is "taking anti-anglers seriously". Anti-angling propaganda is often absurd beyond belief. Anglers know this and dismiss it. But what about the non-anglers? If things come politically to a head it's the non-anglers who will carry the day. Those that are against angling won't change their minds but those in the neutral corner can be won over. Gaining sympathies and votes is, apart from emotional appeals, largely dependent on the right arguments. If anglers bury their heads in the sand in the hope that the storm might blow over they might be in for a surprise: when the heads come up again angling will have been banned. The writing is on the wall. I fully agree with Graham Marsden, Editor of Graham Marsden's *Angling Magazine* (online), who highlights the heart of the matter in an article on the banning of keepnets:

Let's not ban something simply because we don't approve of it, especially when what we want to ditch gives more pleasure to others than ourselves. Banning anything is usually a case of taking the easy way out, by someone who has no use for it himself. Let's continue to improve on retaining systems and educate more in their use. Perhaps there is a case for restricting the use of keepnets to certain fisheries, and for certain species, but to ban something completely, when it is not a vital part of your own pleasure, is selfish and, in this instance, short-sighted, for I believe that a great many anglers would give up fishing if keepnets were banned for everything except match fishing. That would be a massive blow to the sport as a whole.

14

Above all, avoid the silly argument that something or other 'does not do the fish any good.' The very essence of angling, that of pulling a hook into a fish's mouth and hauling it struggling from the water, does not do the fish any good either. We should never lose sight of that whenever we argue against what is harmful to fish. There is an enormous difference between something that does not do any harm and something that does not do any good.

The all burning question we should ask ourselves, when considering banning any angling activity, is this: at what point do we begin to defend our sport? Every single ban is an erosion of our right to fish. The more something is eroded the weaker it becomes. You may not like live-baiting, you may not like bolt-rigs, or hair-rigs, or keepnets. But there will be anglers out there who will leave the sport if those choices are removed. Removing keepnets, I'm convinced, would effectively remove a great many anglers. Can we afford to do that?

Again, please don't use the thoughtless argument that keepnets don't do fish any good, for there are 101 activities in angling that applies to. The main one being the act of penetrating the fish's lip with cold steel and dragging it from the water. How do we defend that activity, the ultimate angling act, when we cannot defend retaining a fish in a net?

Apart from anything else I truly believe that the non-angling public see keepnets as the coarse fisherman's symbol that we care for fish; the symbol that we return them to the water rather than knock them on the head. Again I must ask: at what point do we begin to defend our sport? Only when the basic act of hooking and landing fish is left? And only then on horrendously expensive biodegradable lines with methods and baits approved by who-knows-what authority? But only until fishing is banned altogether of course.[2]

That leads to the second point about giving publicity to the anti-anglers. If there is one thing the angling opponents are excellent at it's

2 Graham Marsden, "Keepnets – do we need them?"
http://www.cygnet.co.uk/ukfw/gmarsd/keepnet.html

publicity. The little bit I might add by discussing the ethics of angling is insignificant and I'm certainly not waking up sleeping dogs. The animal rights movement is as active as it ever was. The evidence can be found in the papers and the news every day.

The great march of the Countryside Alliance on 22 September 2002 in London was in a way the most dramatic illustration of how far animal rights ideas have penetrated the political establishment. The threatened ban on traditional fox hunting shows just how successful and influential animal rights ideas, often in the guise of animal welfare, have become. More than 400,000 people felt compelled to react against a situation and plans which undermine their way of life and their livelihood. At the bottom of anti-hunting and anti-angling is the concept of animal rights. A ban on traditional hunting, partial or total, is the first nail in the coffin of country life and traditional values. That is why non-hunters also feel strongly about it.

It is only a matter of time before angling will be taken on (again). It might not be a head-on confrontation but some clever piecemeal tactics may be focusing on a minor aspect, as in the case of the keepnet. Although nobody knows when and where and in which country the next systematic attack will be launched, it certainly doesn't harm to know on what grounds angling will come under fire. The arguments of the anti-anglers for abolishing angling are the same everywhere. Basically the same also are the angler's interests – coarse angler, sea angler and fly fisherman are in the same boat. If angling is going to be banned, it's all angling. If one type of angling is seen to be wrong, so must all types.

To my knowledge there is very little ethical literature written by fishermen on the subject of fishing. That's extraordinary and I can only assume that those people in a position to write it don't see the urgency of doing so or, more realistically, fear that too much fishing time would be sacrificed. Maybe professional philosophers who are anglers abstain from the topic because it doesn't tie in with their particular field of academic interest; or maybe they feel they would expose themselves too much in the present academic climate. Maybe there aren't any fisher philosophers.

Hook, Line and Thinker, like many books on angling, draws also on personal experience. The personal angle adds spice. Poetry is part of that angle. As I am partial to angling I try always to keep the following lines by William Wordsworth in the back of my mind:

16

A narrow girdle of rough stones and crags,
A rude and natural causeway, interposed
Between the water and a winding slope
Of copse and thicket, leaves the eastern shore
Of Grasmere safe in its own privacy:
And there myself and two beloved Friends,
One calm September morning, ere the mist
Had altogether yielded to the sun,
Sauntered on this retired and difficult way.
—— Ill suits the road with one in haste; but we
Played with our time; and, as we strolled along,
It was our occupation to observe
Such objects as the waves had tossed ashore –
Feather, or leaf, or weed, or withered bough,
Each on the other heaped, along the line
Of the dry wreck. And, in our vacant mood,
Not seldom did we stop to watch some tuft
Of dandelion seed or thistle beard,
Which, seeming lifeless half, and half impelled
By some internal feeling, skimmed along
Close to the surface of the lake that lay
Asleep in a dead calm, ran closely on
Along the dead calm lake, now here now there,
In all its sportive wanderings, all the while,
Making report of an invisible breeze
That was its wings, its chariot, and its horse,
Its playmate, rather say its moving soul.
—— And often, trifling with a privilege
Alike indulged to all, we paused, one now,
And now the other, to point out, perchance
To pluck, some flower or water weed, too fair
Either to be divided from the place
On which it grew, or to be left alone
To its own beauty. Many such there are,
Fair ferns and flowers, and chiefly that tall fern,
So stately of queen Osmunda named;
Plant lovelier, in its own retire abode
On Grasmere's beach, than Naiad by the side
Of Grecian brook, or Lady of the Mere,

Sole-sitting by the shores of old romance.
So fared we that bright morning: from the fields
Meanwhile, a noise was heard, the busy mirth
Of reapers, men and women, boys and girls.
Delighted much to listen to those sounds,
And feeding thus our fancies, we advanced
Along the indented shore; when suddenly,
Through a thin veil of glittering haze was seen
Before us, on a point of jutting land,
The tall and upright figure of a Man
Attired in peasant's garb, who stood alone,
Angling beside the margin of the lake.
That way we turned our steps; nor was it long,
Ere making ready comments on the sight
Which then we saw, with one and the same voice
We all cried out, that he must be indeed
An idle man who thus can lose a day
Of the mid harvest, when the labourers' hire
Is ample, and some little might be stored
Wherewith to cheer him in winter time.
Thus talking of that Peasant, we approached
Close to the spot where with his rod and line
He stood alone; whereat he turned his head
To greet us — and we saw a Man worn down
By sickness, gaunt and lean, with sunken cheeks
And wasted limbs, his legs so long and lean
That for my single self I looked at them,
Forgetful of the body they sustained.
Too weak to labour in the harvest field,
The Man was using his best skill to gain
A pittance from the dead unfeeling lake
That knew not of his wants. I will not say
What thoughts immediately were ours, nor how
The happy idleness of that sweet morn,
With all its lovely images, was changed
To serious musing and self-reproach.
Nor did we fail to see within ourselves
What need there is to be reserved in speech,
And temper all our thoughts with charity.
Therefore unwilling to forget that day,

My Friend, Myself, and She who then received
The same admonishment, have called the place
By a memorial name, uncouth indeed
As e'er by mariner was given to bay
Or Foreland, on a new discovered coast;
And POINT RASH-JUDGEMENT is the name it bears.[3]

The notable exception concerning writing on ethics and angling is A.A. Luce with his most beautiful and inspiring book *Fishing and Thinking*,[4] a landmark in angling literature. In Luce's day the discussion, if indeed there was any, pivoted around the problem of cruelty:

> *... if angling be intrinsically cruel, we anglers, all of us, are doing and encouraging what is intrinsically wrong.*
> *Some readers may feel disposed to brush the charge aside without more ado. They like fishing; it never did them any harm; their fathers and grandfathers before them fished; it is in the blood, and there are many worse ways of spending a day. Fishing keeps the lads out of mischief. Why bother about a handful of dismal croakers who cannot catch fish themselves, and grudge us our amusement? Those who fish and think will not be satisfied with any such reply.*[5]

Since its first publication in 1959 the situation for anglers has dramatically changed. Fishermen face on top of the central and specific cruelty charges the more general and insidious accusation of violating the rights of animals. (Animal rights: the assumption that animals have rights in the same way as human beings.) There is even a "Universal Declaration of Animal Rights" which, of course, denies human beings a right to fish and hunt. Consider Article 10 of this declaration:

> *Educational and schooling authorities must ensure that citizens learn from childhood to observe, understand and respect animals.*[6]

---

3 William Wordsworth, *The Major Works*, "Poems on the Naming of Places IV", Oxford University Press (2000) p.203.
4 A.A. Luce, *Fishing and Thinking*, Swan Hill Press, Shrewsbury, England (1990), p.170. There is also, of course, *Confessions of a Shooting Fishing Man*, by Laurence Catlow (Merlin Unwin Books, Ludlow, England, 1996). This addresses some of the issues. There are a few pages here and there like in *Fly Fishing for Sharks* by Richard Louv (Simon & Schuster, New York, 2000) and in articles scattered in the world's angling press.
5 Ibid., p.170.
6 http://league-animal-rights.org/duda_a.htm

This is the blueprint for large-scale brainwashing. Fundamental societal change is indeed what the leading animal rights philosophers and their zealots have in mind. The envisaged uprooting of traditional values is so radical that only the totalitarian experiences of the 20th century qualify for comparison. Along the way to a "cruelty-free" world, hunters and fishermen will be among the first victims. Do I unduly exaggerate? Anglers never do. No – from the lofty academic heights down to the grass roots level the vanguard of the animal rights movement is already with us.

That trade fair lasted two days and two days of shouting yourself hoarse needs some doing. Full marks for perseverance.

Chapter 1

SHORT CUT

"Fishing is good" is a statement of fact and a moral judgement. Fishing used to be unquestionably good until it became a moral issue with the advent of animal rights ideas. The reason ethics is paramount to angling is simply that if the animal rights philosophers and their influential supporters get their way, then restrictions on angling are the beginning and banning is the end. Ethics, or moral philosophy, is the systematic study and application of the ideas and concepts governing actions and attitudes in relation to right and wrong and good and bad.

Choice is a necessary condition for there to be an ethical discussion in the first place. Some exponents of the theory of evolution would question the existence of human free will. The argument is that all our actions are governed by genes and that the meaning of human life and evolution is to ensure the survival of our genes. Should you meet somebody who objects to your angling and who turns out to believe that life is but the passing on of genes and that genes determine our actions you don't need to pursue the matter further. As there are no ethics involved, there is no point in discussing them.

Evolution is presently the universal scientific currency. The theory of evolution says that all present life developed and branched out from a primaeval soup. Over time different forms of life came into being and disappeared again. Natural selection is the engine of evolution. If a species adapts successfully to an environment, then there will be optimal reproduction and thus the favourable traits will be passed on. Failure to adapt results in extinction.

The theory of evolution is important in that it is part of the underpinnings of the animal rights theories which seek the abolition of angling. Animal rights philosophers regard man as just another animal in the evolutionary process. Animals, especially primates, are thus seen not just as distant relatives but as brothers – alas without reason, speech or laughter.

On the basis of evolution, animals are attributed an unprecedented degree of humanness. By the same token human beings are seen as brutish as never before. Thus evolution provides a key assumption for granting rights to animals. Although the bare bones of the theory of evolution are undisputed, the theory itself comes in all shapes and guises and is an ongoing scientific concern with a lot of open questions. Animal rightists tend to assume that all questions concerning evolution have already been settled.

The fishing gene

I was still in nappies then but I immediately understood what those men with their long bamboo poles were doing on the river bank. I simply knew that the shiny things at the end of their lines were fish, although I didn't know the word 'fish' then, nor did I have any idea what a float, hook, line or sinker were. At the sight of those men something in me immediately responded to the situation. I was hooked and knew that fishing was what I wanted to do more than anything else. No need for an explanation of what, if you break it down into its components, is a fairly complex activity. This is extraordinary because later on it took me ages to work out much simpler connections, like the one between girls and boys. To this very day I am still convinced, for example, that it is far more gallant to bring home a brace of trout rather than a bunch of flowers.

Only a few years later, at the age of eight, I sat on the river bank with a bamboo pole. Not alone, I had nanny beside me. Knitting. This didn't strike me as particularly fishermanly but I had little say in the matter. She had to take out the permit in her name because the legal fishing age was twelve. Such was my determination and nagging power that my parents consented to this unusual arrangement. Technically speaking I wasn't even allowed to fish, I was poaching in a way because it was nanny who had permission to fish. The bailiff probably turned a blind eye because he must have seen that, despite my keenness, it would take a while before I would catch fish. Nanny was knitting and watching and I was left to my own fishing devices.

John Locke, the great 17th century English philosopher, would reject my account of turning from an ordinary toddler into a fishing child. Or at least he would modify it substantially because he held that the mind was a blank page on which only experience and learning could write the story of the self, of language and knowledge. There are no innate ideas. In modern parlance the brain at birth isn't equipped with programs that set themselves up automatically upon receiving the relevant signal (bamboo poles, shiny objects). Experience, according to Locke and other empiricists, is the sole source of knowledge. That experience baby Alexander could have gained from previous excursions to the river in the pram. When I understood what was going on I put two and two together on the basis of previous experience. Sounds straightforward and simple, but it isn't: how experience and the mind interact, how knowledge gets there, puzzles the best brains. Wordsworth highlights the problem with poetical clarity:

Those incidental charms which first attached
My heart to rural objects, day by day
Grew weaker, and I hasten on to tell
How Nature, intervenient till this time,
And secondary, now at length was sought
For her own sake. But who shall parcel out
His Intellect, by geometric rules,
Split, like a province, into round and square?
Who knows the individual hour in which
His habits were first sown, even as a seed,
Who that shall point, as with a wand, and say,
'This portion of the river of my mind
Came from yon fountain?' ... [7]

Edward O. Wilson for one points with a wand and tells us when and why your habits were first sown:

The newly fertilised egg, a corpuscle one two-hundredth of an inch in diameter, is not a human being. It is a set of instructions sent floating into the cavity of the womb. Enfolded within its spherical nucleus are an estimated 250 thousand or more pairs of genes, of which fifty thousand will direct the assembly of the proteins and the remainder will regulate their rates of development. [8]

The human mind developing out of conception:

... is not a tabula rasa, a clean slate on which experience draws intricate pictures with lines and dots. [9]

---

7 William Wordsworth, *The Major Works*, "Prelude Book II", p.397.
8 Edward O. Wilson, *On Human Nature*, Harvard University Press, 2001, p.53. Presently the number of genes is hotly disputed. Estimates range from 27,462 to 153,478. (http://news.bbc.co.uk/1/hi/sci/tech/1426702.stm).
9 Ibid., p.67.

According to this fishing was in my genes and was placed there by evolution. The genes are our evolutionary fate and the function of the intellect is to promote the survival of human genes. The meaning-of-life-question is thus simply answered: it's all about passing on genes. The body is a gene container, so to speak. That's all there is to it because:

...the species lacks any goal external to its own biological nature[10]

This line of thinking or rather interpreting certain facts leads in the extreme version to a full-blooded genetic determinism. We are

...created by the interaction of the genes and the environment. It would appear that our freedom is only self-delusion.[11]

If this were indeed the case, the mind – the 'you' really – is a complete mirage. The mind is a swindler. It leads you to believe, for example, that you have choices. You haven't, your actions are determined by chemical processes in the brain which are controlled by programmed predispositions. These in turn originate in genes. Furthermore the genes themselves are governed by chemical processes and these in turn by particle physics. In the final analysis it's electrons and protons or whatever. This is why such a view is called materialism. Matter is all that matters.

In determinism, it's not you that is doing the doing. You're only led to believe that this is so. So in a way you're doing the doing all the same because somebody or something has to do the believing. Paradox, but there you are.[12] The vital point however is that with such a view, based on the theory of evolution, there isn't really freedom of choice regarding human actions. If this is in fact the case, there can be no moral issue about fishing, none whatsoever. You do what you have to do and that's it – never mind rights, consequences, whatever. No choice, no ethics.

10 Ibid., p.3.
11 Ibid., p.71.
12 This is simplifying matters a bit and it is not Wilson's view, I believe, but he certainly flirts with it at the beginning of Chapter 4, "Emergence".

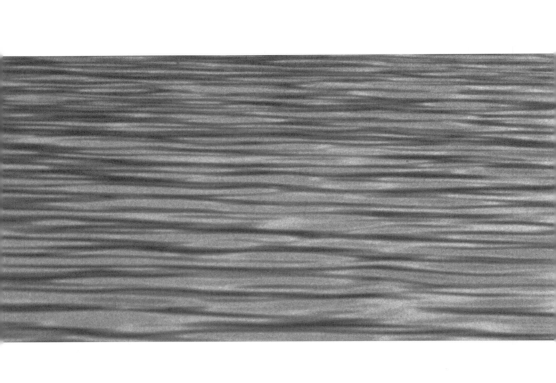

Dear fellow biomasses

I t's a long story. Very long: according to the Big Bang Theory the universe came into being 10 to 20 billion years ago. The birth of the sun is dated to 5 billion years ago and the first life forms are said to have developed 3.5 billion years ago. These were cells from which all future life stemmed. Or if you prefer to look at it from the other side: all present life forms, including human beings, originated in those simple organisms. The first fish fossils are traced to a time called Ordovician which was about 500 million years ago. The oldest known fishing hooks were used 8,000 to 10,000 years ago,[13] and the first written evidence on fly fishing dates back to between AD 41 and AD 104.[14]

The theory of evolution is present-day universal currency in the scientific community. The outline of the original theory by Charles Darwin is beautifully simple and reads something like this:

1. All present life forms, all present species, have developed from earlier forms of life.

2. Along the evolutionary line some new species appear, some others become extinct. Evolution is permanent change over incredibly long time spans. Fossils are the record of change.

3. The mechanism of evolutionary change is natural selection. Natural selection is a process whereby those organisms best able to adapt to their given environment will reproduce best and thereby pass on their successful traits to future generations.

The Origin of Species was first published in 1859. Today's mass of supporting evidence, knowledge and ingenious explanations for all sorts of things is overwhelming. Darwinism is omnipresent and as popular as can be. No conversation or discussion about nature or animals lacks a dash of

---

13 http://www.mustad.no/history/hook_history.html
14 Andrew Herd, *The Fly*, The Medlar Press Ltd, Ellesmere, England (2001), pp.22–23.

Darwinism, explicitly or implicitly. No scientific idea probably has ever penetrated and indoctrinated Western society more than Darwinism. Give it another generation or two and even genes will be convinced. Genes are at the helm of evolution. The "traits" in the preceding definition are nothing other than genes at work. You and I inherited our genes and there is, according to full-blooded genetic determinism, nothing you can do about it. That urge to go fishing is not innocent escapism but your genes telling you what to do. Now, there's an excuse for going fishing as good as any.

Evolution as a word passes the lips easily. If the very word had been a bit trickier, something like "antidisestablishmentarianism," people might think twice before using it. However, everybody is happily employing the term to bolster up an argument or to give one's theories a scientific tinge. It's like football: everybody is an expert. Everybody feels called to explain everything.

Let's have a look at some present-day scientific activity closely tied to the evolutionary idea. Very popular with scientists and the public is research which focuses on partner selection, sex and beauty:

> *... nature cares nothing for appearances, except in so far as they may be useful to any being.*[15]

In a fascinating article entitled "Sexual Selection and the Biology of Beauty" the author enquires into the function of beauty. The extract reads as follows:

> *Sexual selection arises from the advantages that individuals have over others of the same sex and species in mating competition for reproduction. This process may give rise to extravagant sexual characters that are directly detrimental to survival, but beneficial to mating success. Current theoretical and empirical findings suggest that mate preferences are mainly cued in on health including developmental health. Beautiful irresistible features have evolved numerous times in plants and animals due to the immense selection pressures mainly caused by females, and such preferences and beauty standards provide evidence for the claim that human beauty and obsession with bodily beauty equals similar tendencies*

15 Darwin, *The Origin of Species*, Bantam Books, New York (1999), p.70.

throughout the plant and animal kingdoms. The beauty, cosmetics and plastic surgery industries are therefore only surface phenomena that support this evolutionary interpretation. Human beauty standards reflect our evolutionary distant and recent past and emphasise the role of health assessment in mate choice. Given these findings, it is extremely unlikely that human sexual behaviour or mate preference will change to any significant degree during the future, even in the presence of totalitarian measures. [16]

The problem with research like this is not that it lacks purpose or interest. It's more that following it gets hard at times. Faced with the complex findings and fiendishly clever explanations of scientists, the layman is left bewildered. He isn't alone, though. I doubt whether in this vast business of evolutionary science anybody is still able to distinguish fact from fiction.

The popular beauty-health equation, for example, is certainly not above suspicion: how come, over millions of years, there are still genetically unhealthy people, if nature indeed selects for health? And why are beauty and health often found so wide apart?

It might be objected that notable exceptions are statistical aberrations. If not, auxiliary research is required to buttress the original case, ad infinitum, with the result that there will be millions and millions and millions of evolutionary explanations for the most banal or obscure actions or traits in humans or animals. But where shall wisdom be found?

The bare bones of evolutionary theory as outlined above are accepted by all who subscribe to evolution. From there on it's the jungle, with various schools struggling for survival. The most fundamental dispute is between those who claim that God had a hand in it and their opponents who won't hear of that. Even among those of either subgroup there are some lively discussions going on about the works of evolution. The whole evolutionary enterprise seems to be in the process of losing the wood for the trees. In a slightly different but nevertheless pertinent context, Erwin Chargaff writes:

One consequence of sudden bigness, of the abrupt swelling of science, has been the enormous increase in the number of publications. Many new

16 Anders Pape Møller, "Sexual Selection and the Biology of Beauty",
http://www.mindship.org/moller.htm

journals arose, mostly serving special interests. As the brain of man has changed much less than his habitat, a form of scientific neurosis has come about which no longer permits the individual scientist to stand firmly on the ground; he floats, weightless as it were, in a wide space, buffeted by forces he does not understand any more. The production of scientific knowledge on the assembly line has diminished or abolished the value of knowledge itself. Just as our powers of perception are geared to a definite rhythm at which sensations can be apprehended, an increase in the speed with which scientific knowledge is produced can only cause dizziness or, alternatively, a protective encapsulation of the individual. These changes have led to a tremendous fragmentation of all scientific disciplines into a host of mutually unintelligible cliques.[17]

Another point to note is the effortless glide of evolutionary language between the worlds of plants, animals and man. And why not? After all it is claimed that all life originated in a sort of primaeval soup. The day scientists will address each other with "Dear learned fellow animals", "Dear fellow gene carriers" or "My honourable digestive tube" is certainly not far off. After all "colleagues" and "friends" are probably too human as terms, there's a bias in them, and they don't obviously convey that we are animals. If you push this terminological fancy a bit further you'll end up with Prime Ministers or Presidents of nations addressing their people as "Dear fellow citizens and other animals" or ultimately "Dear fellow biomasses". The first chapter of Richard Dawkins' much hailed book, The Blind Watchmaker, opens with an impressive salvo:

We animals are the most complicated things in the known universe.[18]

Primates fascinate scientists because these are apparently our closest relatives. Frans B.M. de Waal, a prolific writer and well-known authority on the subject has studied bonobos. Bonobos are great apes today found only in the tropical forests of the Congo basin. "Bonobo Sex and Society" is the promising title of a captivating article. The bonobo, according de Waal:

...shares more than 98 percent of our genetic profile, making it as close to a human as, say, a fox is to a dog.[19]

17 http://crystal.biochem.queensv.ca/forsdyke/bioinfo1.htm
18 Richard Dawkins, *The Blind Watchmaker*, W.W. Norton & Company (1996) p.1.
19 Frans B.M. de Waal, *Scientific American*, "Bonobo Sex and Society", (March 1995), pp.82–88.

Then follows a description and analysis of the bonobo sex life which, exciting as it most certainly is, we will skip and head directly for the conclusion:

The bonobo's behavioral peculiarities may help us understand the role of sex and may have serious implications for models of human society.
Just imagine that we had never heard of chimpanzees or baboons and had known bonobos first. We would at present most likely believe that early hominids lived in female-centered societies, in which sex served important social functions and in which warfare was rare or absent. In the end, perhaps the most successful reconstruction of our past will be based not on chimpanzees or even on bonobos but on a three-way comparison of chimpanzees, bonobos and humans.[20]

This 98% sounds really impressive. But what does it mean, apart from seducing the reader into thinking that apes are almost human or humans almost apes? You have probably never heard of that tiny microscopic worm called the nematode. These are extraordinary little creatures and are said to share 63% of our genetic profile. With baker's yeast we are apparently genetically related to the degree of 38%. What does this mean and why can't we learn something significant about our past from nematodes and bakers yeast? Surely 63% and 38% are close enough? Apart from that, is the human in the worm really 63% and if so, why doesn't the worm look two-thirds human? Does genetic similarity mean anything at all?

Deoxyribonucleic acid, DNA, is the substance which transmits genetic information. If all life has evolved out of the same primaeval soup it isn't surprising that all life forms share some degree of genetical relationship which will show in DNA comparisons. Knowing in fact still very little about what that common 98% of DNA in apes and human beings is all about, what precise information it carries and how this all works, it seems presumptuous to make comparisons without reservations. Yet Darwinists often pretend all is known, all makes sense. The time-honoured advice of not counting your chickens before they are hatched is frequently thrown to the wind for the sake of scientific glory, publicity and money. That 98% is a smokescreen

20 Ibid.

hiding what in essence is still speculation about vast unknown areas.[21] And as for precision in general it is just as well to remember that scientists presently cannot even agree on the number of human genes: estimates vary between 27,462 and 153,478 which isn't exactly confidence-inspiring.[22] The estimates however are precise: 62 not 63, 78 not 79...

The situation with the remaining 2% is even more telling: what a difference it makes! To all practical purposes it sets apes and human beings worlds apart. Apes don't speak, they don't laugh, they don't pray, they don't play guitar, they don't paint pictures, they don't philosophise, they don't fish, they don't play football, they don't... They don't know duties or obligations – in fact to all intents and purposes they are as different as can be from human beings. Nevertheless there are scores of scientists and animal rights philosophers bending over backwards to show that they are really quite the same as we are and that they should enjoy the same rights as human beings.

Anybody doubting the 98% similarity assumption by not taking it at face value has had a hard time in the last 30 years. By emphasising the difference between man and animals, especially apes, many serious philosophers have been made the target of ridicule by animal rightists. The latest research in evolutionary genetics now shows that man and ape are not that similar after all. The 98% dogma is subject to revision.[23]

A perspicacious, incisive and refreshingly sober angle on the ape hype is presented by Jonathan Marks:

Given a human and a chimpanzee, you can easily tell them apart, but given only their DNA, you can't tell them apart.
But there is a bias of history here. We've been studying chimpanzees for 300 years, but DNA sequences for barely 20 years. We are far more

---

21 There is also the problem of so-called "junk" DNA. Junk DNA is DNA that is said not to be genetically active. But which DNA exactly is junk, if indeed there is junk, at present nobody knows. The closer you look at the problems of genetic science the more you realise how little is known for certain. Pretending that the whole genetic and with it the evolutionary story is crystal clear is helpful in philosophical arguments in as much as it seems to make them "scientific" and with that beyond questioning. Typically Singer, for example, claims :"We are the first generation to understand not only that we have evolved, but also the mechanism by which we have evolved and how this evolutionary heritage influences our behaviour." (Peter Singer, *A Darwinian Left*, p.63.)
22 http://news.bbc.co.uk/1/hi/sci/tech/1426702.stm
23 *Science*, Vol. 298, 25 October 2002, pp.719–721.

familiar with apes than we are with DNA. Consequently, the appropriate way to compare this data is not to contrast the genetic and anatomical comparisons through modern eyes, but to compare the genetics today with the anatomical comparisons when those were as new and as exciting as DNA comparisons are today.

And what you find is that the leading scholars of the 1700s, the leading philosophers, were struck by the overwhelming physical similarity of ape and human. Rousseau and Monboddo were struck by the humanness of the ape and declared it to be a variant human. Linnaeus famously classified the apes as both Homo troglodytes or nocturnus – a different kind of human – and as Simia satyrus a different kind of monkey.

So the point I wish to make is that the paradox of the anatomical difference and the genetical similarity is illusory – it's an artefact of the intellectual history of comparing. How familiar we are at the turn of the millennium with the physical differences and how unfamiliar we are with the whole notion of genetic difference. [24]

There is an uncanny obsession with great apes in some circles. Regardless of the facts, they have to be humanised at all costs. Some of these great apes like Washoe, Koko and Lucy have attained such a level of fame in animal rights literature that some academics probably wouldn't mind if they were conferred with honorary doctoral degrees. No self-respecting publication in the domain of animal rights philosophy can do without reference to the primates and a bit of campaigning for

giving apes the same legal rights as children and mentally retarded adults. [25]

So much for the evolutionary framework. Back to ethics. Ethics has a place in evolution. Obviously, because all human societies (in contrast to animal "societies") are governed by some ideas about morals, about dos and don'ts. Attempts have been made to explain ethics in evolutionary terms purely as a function of the process of adaptation. This leads inevitably back to determinism. We have already seen that if we are the slaves of our genes,

24 Jonathan Marks, "What It Really Means To Be 99% Chimpanzee", presented at the Annual Meeting of the American Anthropological Association, November 20, 1999.
25 http://www.psyeta.org / This is the website of "Psychologists for the ethical treatment of animals". The motto of this organisation is: "Using psychology and education to enrich the world through respect for human and non-human animals."

our choices are not really choices at all. A closer look will however show that even if the genes are choosing there is ethics.

The genes might not literally order or cunningly cause you to do X rather than Y in a situation but they do definitely dispose you to do X rather than Y. Like fishing or knitting. There is no real freedom of choice – we execute whatever is demanded of us by the interest of the genes because we are their survival vehicles and not autonomous beings. This, if true, drains the meaning out of every moral discussion. Ethics and all other human endeavours are make-believe, pretending at the same that they aren't. The scope of such a state of affairs is all embracing: logic isn't really logic anymore. Even mathematics or physics, which usually stand firm as a rock against the storms of lofty theories, are nothing but deceptive ploys of the genes. Since we are human, the standard is human. Mathematical and physical laws make sense to human beings, i.e. the survival vehicles for the genes. Beyond that they are meaningless.

Trying to be virtuous, leading a good life and all things traditionally associated with morals are nothing more than the genes at work because these actions enhance the chances for the genes' perpetuity. If we strip all the decorum away from what people are and do, all there is left of ethics and life are biomasses (human beings) trying to get the best deal possible for their genes.

It is, I believe, not half as bad. There is free will, although it's true that we don't have a choice about our being – in the most elementary sense we can't choose who we want to be, and where we want to be. For all practical purposes it is, however, the case that we can and do make choices. It's straightforward really and no mystery – regardless of genetic programming or physical laws. It's your day off, for example, it's early September and you try to decide whether or not you should go mushroom stalking or fishing. There's nothing and nobody to influence or constrain you, there is just you, your knowledge, reason, and a hunch about what could be going on where. You might decide both ways: going fishing in the morning and mushroom stalking in the afternoon. But whatever you decide to do it's a free choice within the given context. The subsequent actions and the consequences thereof are your responsibility. In the absence of force or constraint and in full presence of your deliberating powers, there is choice.

We are not free to will everything we could want, like being somebody else, but we are in principle free to do what we want. And this entails responsibility and with it ethical questions about the criteria which help us to deliberate. Evolution or no evolution, genes or no genes: ethics are here to stay.

There is a compulsion however. I had to go fishing recently in high summer. It had been a day vibrant with heat and I had a hunch that towards the evening there might be some perch action down at the river. It looked promising there, just in front of that reed bed. The river banks were shrubby, interspersed with reed patches. Good cover. Before my first cast I spotted a fellow angler on the other bank. Maybe 50 yards upstream from where I stood. I didn't actually see him; what I saw was his rod above the shrubs and reeds when he cast and retrieved and the float when on the water. Somebody else with a hunch. I baited the hook with a lively worm from rabbit manure – the connoisseur's choice. The perch shared my predilection. I didn't have to wait long to see the float dart off in perchy fashion. A rumble in the distance and low-flying swallows accompanied the landing of the first perch. Looking upstream, I saw my fellow angler's rod also in action. Great. More rumbling louder and closer. The thunderstorm approached with seven-league boots. Never mind, I thought, the going is good and as long as that guy fishes, I'll stay as well. Strange how one sometimes abandons reason and delegates responsibility – was it greed that made me stay there glued to the river bank? I caught another two perch.

Although I could clearly see this kingsize thunderstorm approaching, I didn't budge. Stupid. I continued fishing as long as I could see that rod upstream. This meant exposing myself to the elements which within minutes threw everything it had at me. When finally that rod disappeared from sight, it did so in a shower of hail. The pellets were of tennis ball size so that I had to shelter under a tree. In a second wave, rain followed – a tropical downpour. By the time I reached the car I was soaked and cursing myself for this pointless one-upmanship. That I have to go fishing doesn't mean I have to go fishing stupidly. There is freedom not to fish stupidly! There's that – and a postscript: a couple of days later I met a few fishermen in the pub. The conversation turned to that thunderstorm which had left a newsworthy trail of damage in its wake. One of the anglers described the storm in vivid detail and when asked why he kept on fishing under such dangerous, ultimately hopeless conditions, answered: "Well, you see, there was this guy about 50 yards downstream from me, I couldn't see him really, just his rod … I thought as long as that idiot downstream keeps fishing I'll stay as well." The laughter prompted by the revelation that I was the idiot in question almost brought the roof of the pub down.

Intermezzo

A word of warning: today practically everybody in philosophy and the social sciences seems to be an expert in evolution, biology, bioarchaeology, zoology, evolutionary psychology, ethology, sociobiology, ecology, deep ecology, biopsychology, bioastronautics, biohistory, bioethics, ecofeminism, genomics, genetics etc. Often, and on top of all these, there's also chemistry, physics and mathematics. I just wonder whether all the people who so confidently bandy about scientific slang actually understand what they are saying.[26] If you get involved in a discussion about angling, always try to check whether the person you are dealing with actually has an idea about what he is saying. Just ask the simple questions a child would ask. Why? What exactly is such and such? It won't make you popular but you will discover soon how well-founded the anti-angler's propaganda package is.

People often say that animals have rights, such as not to be cruelly treated. But what many people mean when they say 'rights' is in fact 'welfare'. Animal rights and animal welfare are two utterly different concepts. 'Animal rights' means exactly what it says, i.e. giving animals the same moral and legal rights as human beings. 'Animal welfare' by contrast is

---

26 See *Impostures Intellectuelles* by Alan Sokal and Jean Bricmont, Editions Odile Jacob, Paris, 1997.

the notion that we have a moral duty to care for animals, to prevent cruelty and to look critically at how they are used. The fact that we have moral duties towards animals in no way implies that animals have rights. The source of a moral duty is not necessarily a right on the part of the thing, being or person to which the duty is owed. It is, for example, everyone's duty to avoid wanton waste. The source of this duty is certainly not a right by the waste not to be produced. Or, take the person who saves the runt of the litter from certain death by starvation: the moment he starts feeding the little dog, there is an obligation to look after it, but that in no way signifies that the dog has a right. I don't discuss animal welfare because it is applied wisdom whereas the debate about animal rights is about the fundamental aspects of the relationship between man and beast, fisherman and fish.

Before we take the plunge it is necessary to define what angling is. There are also a lot of people who pretend to know and understand what angling is all about – notably those who want to ban it. In fact, in the strict sense of the word it's really simple: angling is fishing with rod, line and hook as opposed to, for example, spearing or netting. This is fishing in the narrow sense. In a wider sense, to a fisherman, fishing is everything. Almost.

Chapter 2

Animal rights and animal liberation both spell the end of angling and the beginning of vegetarianism. Philosophically speaking, Tom Regan, author of *The Case for Animal Rights*, and Peter Singer, author of *Animal Liberation*, are however worlds apart. The situation is reminiscent of that famous Halford–Skues dispute: but does it really matter to the trout whether it falls to a Halford-style dry fly or to a Skues-style nymph?

Ethics is, broadly speaking, divided into two schools of thinking. There are those who say that the morality of an action is determined by its motive (intention, attitude). The appraisal of an action is in terms of good and bad intentions. The opposing school denies the primacy of motive. It focuses on the consequences of an action and appraisal of it is in terms of right and wrong. This is called "consequentialism". One of the many bones of contention between the two schools is rights. Moral rights. While the non-consequentialist says there are such rights, the consequentialist denies this.

Tom Regan, the world's leading advocate of animal rights, claims that animals have rights even though they can't recognise them in themselves or others. They can't participate in interactions involving rights and duties governed by a free will. The argument runs roughly as follows: evolution is the common source of animals and human beings alike. We're a big family. Animals (especially primates) have a conscience and awareness similar to human beings. This qualifies them, like human beings for the attribution of inherent value which yields in the end moral and legal rights for animals. That's a tall order culminating in saving healthy dogs rather than retarded babies and in the really monstrous assertion that scientists don't have the moral right to experiment

39

with one single rat, even if they are certain that they could save thousands of human lives by doing so. According to Regan, human beings, have

no basic right against nature not to be harmed by those natural diseases we are heir to.[36]

I propose to sponsor identity cards for animal rights activists with that text on it in order to prevent them from being accidentally helped.

Fishing and hunting are, of course, out of the question as they would violate the two basic rights of animals: to be respected and not to be harmed.

Peter Singer, the founding father of the animal rights movement, arrives via a different route at the same conclusion about fishing and hunting. Moral rights are in Singer's philosophy, however, just a convenient short-hand. He doesn't believe in moral rights but in consequences. The rightness of an action depends entirely on the consequences it produces. This is called consequentialism or utilitarianism. Speciesism and equal consideration are the key words for understanding the Singerian story. Speciesism is a

bias in favour of the interests of members of one's own species and against those members of other species.[47]

Speciesism, according to Singer, is the root of all evil and can be overcome by equal consideration. Every being capable of suffering qualifies for equal consideration. Equal consideration means equal moral consideration and eventually legal consideration. Anything that suffers must be treated as the moral equal to a human being. If snails suffer (it is asserted that they do) and speciesism is wrong, then a human baby is on the same moral footing as a snail. Killing perfectly healthy babies, by the way, fits neatly into this line of thinking as we shall see later.

Singer's philosophical credo, called "preference utilitarianism", sees the moral good in the maximisation of people's preferences. The moral good is not a value in the sense of a strict do or don't but a function of people's preferences. Therefore human and animal suffering are not seen as wrong or bad as such but only so in relation to the maximisation of preferences. Strange and confusing as it may seem from somebody who has "Animal Liberation" on his banner, vivisection, for example, or any other kind of suffering inflicted on animals is theoretically permissible because the consequences of it could maximise preferences in a given situation. This moral philosophy is, given the right circumstances, indifferent to human and animal suffering: it's only interested in the logic and arithmetic that govern preferences. Most vividly aware of this confusing inconsistency are anti-vivisectionists, who are at loggerheads with Singer exactly because of it.

Nevertheless Peter Singer remains the leading figure in that conglomerate of deep concern for animals. The reason for this is probably that many people don't bother to understand what Singer is really saying. "Animal Liberation" is a great slogan glossing over the poverty of a philosophy which revels in the wholesale destruction of Western culture. Do I unduly exaggerate? Judge for yourself. Here it is straight from the horse's mouth, so to speak, in Singer's *The Deweese Report*, November 1998:

Christianity is our foe. If animal rights is to succeed, we must destroy the Judeo-Christian religious tradition (see Appendix, Animal Rights Quotes).

Singer wants to sink the Christian and Western moral tradition for good. He doesn't seem to be given to modesty or inhibitions because he has already started to rewrite the biblical commandments. Who else but himself would be in a position to do so? In his book *Thinking about Life and Death* he cheerfully replaces The First old Commandment: "Thou shalt not kill", which implies that all human life is of equal worth, by his First new Commandment:

Recognise that the worth of human life varies

This was fully recognised in the not so distant past. "Unworthy life" were the key words then.

Animal Rights

Long before you're anywhere near water, let alone fish, the potential for landing yourself in trouble is vast. For a start you fortify yourself for the day's fishing ahead with a decent traditional breakfast: bacon, sausage, eggs. On top of that you swat a carnivorous fly which somehow seems intent on having its share. Within minutes you have succeeded in throwing yourself into a moral abyss.

The most prominent advocate of animal rights is Tom Regan. His book, *The Case for Animal Rights* is a punctilious and voluminous work of scholarly philosophy. What is it all about? It starts with a distinction (almost everything in philosophy seems to start with a distinction): Human beings are moral agents; animals are moral patients. Regan explains:

> *Moral patients cannot do what is right or wrong, and in this respect they differ fundamentally from moral agents. But moral patients can be on the receiving end of the right or wrong acts of moral agents, and so in this respect resemble moral agents. A brutal beating administered to a child, for example, is wrong, even if the child herself can do no wrong, just as attending to the basic biological needs of the senile is arguably right, even if a senile person can no longer do what is right. Unlike the case of the relationship that holds between moral agents, then, the relationship that holds between moral agents, on the one hand, and moral patients, on the other, is not reciprocal. Moral patients can do nothing right or wrong that affects or involves moral agents, but moral agents can do what is right or wrong in ways that affect or involve moral patients.* [27]

Ethics or moral philosophy is the study of the principles that govern human action. In order to be a moral agent you have to have a degree of self-consciousness and rationality so that you can understand what is involved when it is said for example that lying is wrong – a bad idea altogether. A moral theory is one which systematises the beliefs and reasons for doing or not doing/believing or not believing one thing or another. The Ten

---

27 Tom Regan, *The Case for Animal Rights*, University of California Press, Berkeley and Los Angeles, CA (1985) p.154.

Commandments are not regarded by many contemporary philosophers as moral theory because they were received from a moral authority: from God.

A moral agent acts in a framework he more or less understands. He can do right or wrong. A moral patient can't. All the same, according to Regan, by virtue of inherent value moral agents and moral patients qualify for moral rights. Moral rights is another term for natural rights – the notion of moral rights is nothing new. Very few things are new in moral philosophy. Anyway:

The principal basic moral right possessed by all moral agents and patients is the right to respectful treatment.[28]

This creates a bond between the two and the moral agent is of course obliged not to violate the moral patient's moral or legal rights. Swatting that fly was probably the most disrespectful thing to do. Worse still, by doing so you ignored the fly's second moral right not to be harmed. It doesn't stop there, but we'll leave it at that.

The question that wants to be answered is why animals (moral patients) qualify for basic moral and legal rights just as humans do (without reciprocity, of course). Evolutionary theory is part of the answer. Humans and animals spring from the same roots. Humans are part of the animal world – we're human animals. Humans and animals are of a kind and so must be their rights. In this light Regan analyses animal behaviour and concludes that animals can be attributed consciousness and other characteristics held to be typically human, such as rationality and a sense of self. This is called animal awareness. It qualifies animals, just as human beings, for inherent value. Inherent value is a postulate. A postulate is a statement which one assumes to be true – it is the basis of a philosophical argument. Value here refers to moral value and means as much as an unconditional good. It's a good in itself. All life, for example, could be said to have inherent value.

The basic moral rights of animals are prima facie rights. Prima facie means "at first glance" in common usage. In legal terminology it means "sufficient in law to establish a case or fact, unless disproved".[29]

28 Ibid., p.327.
29 *Encarta Dictionary*, Microsoft Corporation, USA

This leaves room for manoeuvre as Regan shows in a lifeboat example:

There are five survivors, four normal adult human beings and a dog. The boat will support only four. All will perish if one is not sacrificed.[30]

Regan's answer in this case is unequivocal: the dog[31] must go overboard, but make a note of that word "normal". The reasoning is not that the human animal is more equal than the dog. The death of a normal human weighs heavier than that of the dog, because:

Death for the dog, in short, though a harm, is not comparable to the harm that death would be to any of the humans.[32]

Death is said to be:

a function of the opportunities for satisfaction it forecloses[33]

In this case there would be clearly more opportunities for satisfaction foreclosed if a human were tossed in the drink. Although this makes little sense out of its context, the reason why I mention it is that Regan's view allows for some consideration of human interest over animal interest. In some cases anyway – in others not. When asked in a Q & A session which he would save if a boat capsized in the ocean: a dog, or a baby – he replied:

if it were a retarded baby and a bright dog, I'd save the dog[34]

The retarded baby is not "normal", signifying presumably that death for it would foreclose fewer opportunities than for the dog. How does Regan know the range of a bright dog's opportunities for satisfaction? And how does he know the range of opportunities for retarded people's satisfaction? How can he seriously suggest weighing up entities against each other about which he can't possibly have the faintest idea?

Where's the boundary between normal and retarded (not normal)? How retarded is retarded? How is retardedness assessed and by whom? And how

30 Tom Regan, op.cit., p.351.
31 Ibid., p.351
32 Ibid., p.324.
33 Ibid., p.324.
34 www.furcommission.com   Q&A session following a speech entitled "Animal Rights, Human Wrongs" at the University of Wisconsin-Madison, (October 27, 1989).

hook, line & thinker

bright is bright? Questions of baby killing, unworthy life and euthanasia are never far away when so-called scientifically based philosophies concerning animal rights are discussed. Regan might not be as philosophically fond of death as is his colleague and champion of animal liberation Peter Singer. Nevertheless it can be a fairly rough ride in the wake of Reganite animal rights. Suppose there are good reasons for scientists to believe that one single experiment with a rat could provide the knowledge to cure those afflicted by AIDS. This is what Reganite morals prescribe:

> *Not even a single rat is to be treated as if that animal's value were reducible to his possible utility...*[35]

His view on why using animals in research is categorically out of the question culminates in:

> *We have, then, no basic right against nature not to be harmed by those natural diseases we are heir to.*[36]

Without frills this means you would have to let hundreds of thousands of people die in order to respect one rat's rights. What a message of hope for rats this is!

For human beings it's a bleak picture: nature as the active part inflicts diseases on us to which we have to succumb without even a murmur. What about human ingenuity overcoming difficulties and disease? What about something so profoundly human as hope, what about love? What about the meaning of life beyond conceited fatalism?

No show – nature's iron grip strangles you and rightly so because man is a blot on the earthscape anyway. The problem with stuff like this is that it is earnestly meant to be of universal relevance. Tom Regan doesn't want to accept harm from nature on his own – he sees his philosophy as binding for everybody. Everybody thus is meant to die of fatal diseases that "we are heir to". That such a stance doesn't discredit the author in the eyes of his peers tells a story about the current academic climate and, on the positive side, is irrefutable proof that academic freedom and freedom of expression are in no danger. That is, if you are on the politically correct animal rights side.

---

35 Tom Regan, op.cit., p.384.
36 Ibid., p.388.

46

Opponents of Singer and Regan find it increasingly difficult to get their work published. If they do succeed in making their voices heard they risk being harassed by extremists. Michael Leahy, author of *Against Liberation*,[37] even received death threats.

In the initial discussion Regan confines animal awareness to the higher mammals. He sees the difficulty of where to draw the line between animals that can be said to have self-awareness etc. and others of which this can't be said. There are many differences between a bonobo, a chimp and a snail. The bottom line however is that all animals are equal and therefore of inherent value and thereby at least candidates for moral rights (though, in Orwell's words, some animals may be more equal than others).

Inherent value – moral rights – respectful treatment – the right not to be harmed: the sequence looks impressive. It commands respect, so to speak. Respect is a key to the understanding of all the notions involved in Regan's philosophy. Respect does not mean that you have to bow each time a bee buzzes by or curtsy to every bird. Respect means respect for the law – not primarily for the legal law but for the moral law, the moral rights of, above all, animals.

Let's look at respect. Beyond simply stating that you and I have to respect this, that or the other, Regan isn't really saying much about such a key notion. This might be partly due to the fact that respect, like almost everything in *The Case for Animal Rights* is pouring new wine into old bottles. Respect is the secular version of the Kantian "reverence".[38] A closer look at the concept reveals that respect isn't the clear-cut entity it pretends to be. Respect is a frequently used term for all sorts of relations. There's hardly anything you can't respect. From respecting the law to respecting a tardigrade's dignity (tardigrades are particularly endearing microscopic water animals), anything goes. The underlying idea is that humans, animals and things have, by virtue of their being what they are, a value and that this confers on the being or thing a special status. Reverence is a "complex feeling"[39] said to make us voluntarily abide by whatever precepts follow from the value and the status we recognise. For Kant it was the moral law,

37 Michael Leahy, *Against Liberation – Putting Animals in Perspective*, Routledge, London (1991).
38 H. J. Paton in his translation of the *Grundlegung zur Metaphysik der Sitten* renders the word "Achtung" as "reverence" and not as respect. This is a very subtle and fine point because God has a role to play in the Kantian world. See H. J. Paton, *The Moral Law*, Hutchinson University Library, London (1972).
39 Ibid. There is a concise discussion of Kantian reverence on p.21.

for others it could be human rights or animal rights.

If for example you are given to geological meditations, you might reach the point where you start thinking that the piece of granite you hold in your hand has a value in itself. You begin to see that value in the story of its creation or simply in its beauty. The next step is that you reason inherent values into it and from there you head in a beeline to respect. Like the moral law, the beauty of granite is there because you want it to be there. Reverence (respect) is indeed a "complex feeling".[40] The point to take on board is that respect, like evolution, isn't as straightforward a notion as it appears to be. Always ask what precisely is meant by respect. Incidentally, "dignity" is also a word to watch out for. Inflationary use of "respect" and "dignity" should put you on guard.

The Case for Animal Rights is modelled on Immanuel Kant's *Groundwork of the Metaphysics of Morals*[41] and on John Rawls' *A Theory of Justice*[42]. These are two milestones in the history of philosophy. Regan picks up various strands from both works and weaves them into animal rights. His arguments purportedly prove that there are indeed such rights. One of their implications is vegetarianism i.e. a (moral) duty not to eat meat. Another is that fishing is wrong and so on. Those are the first steps. The fine tuning of these rights and their practical application are an ongoing concern.

Rights entail duties. Animal rights entail duties for human beings only. Animals can't reciprocate and they can't among themselves form a culture of rights or respect because they don't understand those concepts at all. Flummoxing as all this may be, it's far from banal because animal rights, if applied, modify human rights and duties. Consider the example mentioned above: the retarded baby and the bright dog. By conventional moral standards one would save the baby and not the dog. There are many reasons for this, among them a feeling of compassion, the idea that human life is sacred and certainly that the baby, contrary to appearances, does have a chance for a purposeful and meaningful life. Last but not least, when there is no time for intellectually proper and politically correct reflection, one probably intuitively and instinctively tries to save the baby: the life of the baby is simply more important than that of the dog.

---

40 Patrick Pharo, *La Logique du Respect*, Les Editions du Cerf, Paris (2001). This is an excellent introduction to the subject.
41 H.J. Paton, *The Moral Law*, Hutchinson University Library, London (1972).
42 John Rawls, *A Theory of Justice*, Oxford University Press (1972).

On the grounds of animal rights outlined above, vegetarianism is obligatory and, almost needless to say, fishing is an altogether bad idea. Although Regan does not specifically mention fishing, it's reasonable to assume that what he says about hunting also applies to fishing.

The Rights view categorically condemns sport hunting and trapping. [43]

That word "categorical" means there is no room for doubt, contradiction, discussion. Killer! This in a nutshell is the case for animal rights with regard to fishing.

---

43 Tom Regan, op.cit., p351.

Animal Liberation

Peter Singer is, philosophically speaking, a completely different kettle of fish. While Regan is a non-consequentialist, that is, somebody who focuses on rights, Singer is a consequentialist for whom consequences and achieved states of affairs count. Consequentialism holds that it is exclusively the outcome, or the result of an action, that decides between right and wrong. In footballing (soccer) terms Regan wants to win in style, whereas Singer wants to win regardless of the tactics. Contemporary consequentialism is a form of utilitarianism. Utilitarianism is in John Stuart Mill's words:

> the creed which accepts as the foundation of morals, Utility, or the
> Greatest Happiness Principle, holds that actions are right in proportion as
> they tend to promote happiness, wrong as they tend to produce the
> reverse of happiness. By happiness is intended pleasure and the absence
> of pain; by unhappiness, pain and the privation of pleasure.[44]

The so-called utilitarian calculus aims at establishing what in a given set of circumstances is right or wrong. It tries to weigh up what promotes more happiness and/or reduces pain and whatever does the trick is right. This procedure reminds one remarkably of purely commercial thinking. Replace happiness with gain, pleasure with money and pain with loss and you understand its McScrooge appeal immediately.

The Singerian version of the beastie is called "preference utilitarianism". The good resides in the satisfaction of people's preferences and should be maximised. It's a life-style philosophy really. Any fad potentially qualifies for preference.

The moral good is not a value in the sense of a strict do or don't but a function of people's preferences. Therefore human and animal suffering are not seen as wrong or bad as such, but only so in relation to the maximisation

---

44 John Stuart Mill, *Utilitarianism*, Fontana (1974), p.257. John Stuart Mill, 1806–1873, was one of the founding fathers of utilitarianism.

of preferences. Strange as it may seem from somebody who has "Animal Liberation" on his banner, vivisection, for example, or any other kind of animal use is theoretically permissible because the consequences of it could maximise preferences.

Preference utilitarianism is a dithering philosophy which, given the right circumstances, accepts suffering as morally right. Most vividly aware of this confusing possibility are the anti-vivisectionists who are at loggerheads with Singer exactly because of it.[45] Singer can't positively commit himself unequivocally against all animal suffering. His brother-in-arms, yet philosophical opponent, Tom Regan observes with precision:

Singer does not believe that vivisection is always wrong. On the contrary, he believes that it is sometimes right. If the consequences are on balance better than otherwise could be obtained, then his view is that there is nothing wrong with using animals in research. Let me repeat this: his view is there is nothing wrong with using animals in research. This is one way in which I think Singer's ideas are harmful to animals.[46]

This is the sketch of the philosophical background of Peter Singer, the august liberator and hero of the world's animals and their human friends. The root of all evil that Singer discovered back in the Seventies is something he defines as speciesism, which

is a prejudice or attitude of bias in favour of the interests of members of one's own species and against those of members of other species.[47]

That is the one pillar (postulate), the other being that:

the capacity for suffering is the vital characteristic that gives a being the right to equal consideration.[48]

Equal consideration refers to ethics, signifying in consequence that all animals capable of suffering must be included in our moral concepts and

45 See the following websites:
  http://earthsave.bc.ca/animalvoices/singer.htm
  http://www.nzavs.org.nz/34page2.html
46 http://www.animal-lib.org.au/more_interviews/regan/
47 Peter Singer, *Animal Liberation*, Avon Books, New York (1991), p.6. The term was originally coined by Richard Ryder, another prominent advocate of animal rights.
48 Ibid., p.7.

deliberations. This puts the moral relationship between you and your baby daughter on the same footing as that between you and a snail or a shrimp. If the shrimp is capable of suffering and if it's wrong to be speciesist then this is the case – the moral reality according to Singer. Just let the point sink in: your baby daughter has the same moral status as a shrimp. On the arch over the two pillars, is the slogan "ANIMAL LIBERATION" in capital letters. The plight of animals is likened to slavery – what animals experience today is what slaves experienced yesterday.[49]

To the fisherman the consequences of this are the same as in the case of animal rights. Fishing is out of the question. And as you probably already suspected, vegetarianism is just as compulsory.

Singer has a remarkable penchant for topics involving killing and death which earned him the nickname Professor Death. Not surprising really. He discusses killing issues with great gusto. There is something creepy about this fashionable death orientation. There's a morbidness oozing out of some philosophy books that is positively revolting. Whatever happened to life?

The philosophical rift between Regan and Singer is as deep as the Mariana Trench. The fundamental difference is that Regan believes in moral rights whereas Singer wouldn't hear of rights – consequences are his moral stock.

The import for angling and hunting is the same on both accounts: abolition. Deep the rift may be but for all practical purposes it is not very wide. Regan and Singer can shake hands over it. For all the following chapters I use the expression "animal rights", unless otherwise specified, to cover both Regan's and Singer's ideas. This is perfectly in line with the usage by animal rightists, who hail Peter Singer as the father of the Animal Rights Movement.

---

49 Ibid., p.213.

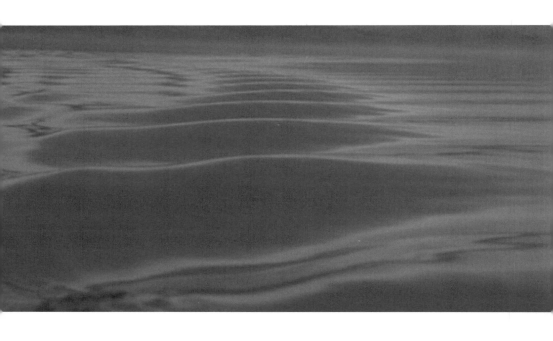

Chapter 3

SHORT CUT

Fishing is often indiscriminately linked to hunting. There are similarities, certainly, but there are also important differences. The fact that fish can and do obstinately refuse to "take", for example, is one such distinguishing characteristic. If the crosshairs are on the hunter's prey, the matter is settled. The accounts of anti-anglers regarding what happens in fishing are often deficient. Well-informed distortion is a popular tactic with philosophers and grass-roots anti-angling activists alike. Fishermen and hunters are, if mentioned together by animal rights advocates, simply classed as cruel. There is a similarity. And it's similarly unqualified.

A common trait in all anti-angling is the bashing of Christianity and Western culture. Animal rightists don't target any one Christian denomination particularly. All persuasions are viewed as detrimental to moral progress and stand in the way of a better world. The very idea of God is a bad idea – for Regan and Singer alike. The Christianity/cruelty-to-animals equation is as popular with animal rightists as it is stupid. The point to note is that the attack on angling goes deeper than it appears. Anti-angling is a facet of a movement that aims to pull the rug from under traditional Western culture.

Jainism takes the basic assumptions of animal rights to their practical and logical limits. Some of the members of this Hinduistic group wear a cloth over nose and mouth so as not to accidentally kill a little insect by breathing. Regan and Singer try to draw lines regarding the rights and consideration granted to animals. This they do so as not to trap themselves in a position like Jainism. The point is, however, that their philosophical and grass-roots followers ignore the line for all practical purposes.

Militant ethical vegetarianism is the proverbial iron fist in a velvet glove. Arson, breaking and entering and the like are in the wake of the Animal Liberation Front and its allies. Should they finally succeed, it will be the end of your fishing and the beginning of your "cruelty-free" diet. *Bon appétit!*

The salmon of wisdom

Angling is often likened to hunting. A. Dionys de Leeuw, who sees no other way than to abandon all sport fishing, does so among other reasons on the grounds that angling is like hunting. He explains that:

> *while hunters make every effort to reduce pain and suffering ... anglers purposefully inflict these conditions on fish.* [50]

And he concludes that because hunting is the same as angling, the same moral justifications have to apply. We'll delve into pain and suffering later. What interests us here is whether angling really is a form of hunting in the full-blooded sense of that word. Consider what is actually happening: the hunter stalks his prey; when it is in range and he is confident he won't miss, he fires. The moment he pulls the trigger the issue is settled for the target. [51] There is no escape and no choice.

Consider now what happens in angling: you spot your fish, you cast for it and it doesn't take! There's no way you can induce a take if the fish doesn't feel like it. You can try, but as every angler knows if the fish has put its fin down not to take it doesn't. Some other day maybe – but not here and now. This applies to all types of angling and fish in all conditions. You can have perfect conditions and no fish, although you know they're there. Even "easy game" like perch can refuse steadfastly. It happens to us all. Even the most skilful master angler now and then is at the end of his wits:

> *There are trout in my river whose attitudes*
> *Are quite of the blackest ingratitude;*
> *Though I offer them duns,*
> *Most superior ones,*
> *They maintain a persistent Black Gnatitude.* [52]

---

50 A. Dionys de Leeuw, *Environmental Ethics*, "Contemplating the Interests of Fish: The Angler's Challenge", p.373.
51 Traditional fox hunting in England is yet another kind of hunting. To get the picture see Roger Scruton, *On Hunting*, St. Augustine Press, South Bend, Indiana (1998).
52 Author unknown.

My first season as a fly fisherman was spent on the banks of the beautiful River Avon[53] in Tomintoul, Scotland. There were a couple of pools from the bridge down to the quarry accessible (affordable) to the public. At the time, I was working for the equally beautiful Dulcinea, who managed the youth hostel. One sunny day with crystal clear water (I wasn't a very experienced salmon angler then, nor am I now) I went down the river. I worked my way up from the quarry to the bridge. In the very last pool before the bridge I spotted the salmon. It would have been difficult to overlook it. It was the monarch not just of that pool but probably of the whole river system. I could hardly believe my eyes – never ever had I seen a fish like it.

I stepped back in surprise. After the first shock had passed I changed leader and fly. The excitement, the hunting fever, was such that I was trembling. I had to make a real effort to calm down, to compose myself, and after a short while it was back to the pool. The salmon was still there. It was lazily basking just a yard or so below the surface. I succeeded reasonably well with my first cast. Somehow, with supreme stupidity and conceitedness, I was for a second convinced the salmon would rise and take as a sort of reward for that well-executed first cast. It didn't. Nor was it convinced by any of the subsequent presentations of various fly patterns. These were nerve-racking moments. After the leviathan actually moved to inspect a Hairy Mary – my heartbeat had soared – just as languidly as it had come up, it went down again. After watching this agape I decided to call it a day.

I reeled in and as I did so a feeling of great anger swept over me as if I were the victim of a great injustice. It's the sort of thinking that because you're such a nice guy and because you're doing everything by the book, fish and fortune should smile on you. They don't, of course; and you shouldn't expect reward for virtue, because virtue is a good in itself. Or is it? Anyway, it's as in real life and I am certain that most will know what "Fishing and the Moral Law in Vermont" by Daniel Cady is all about:

Why is it that them whose morals slant
Can do so much the decent can't?
Jest let a chap his conscience chuck
And generally he plays to luck;

---

53 Avon in Gaelic means River. The River Avon is therefore the "River River".

Erase the line 'twixt right and wrong
And every sob becomes a song –
I s'pose that's why a worthless scout
Can ketch jest twice as many trout.
But still I wouldn't want it spread
That I'm convinced of what I've said;
I offer it for what it's worth
To them that salt and save the earth,
As some excuse and reason why
The fish refuse their worm or fly –
I'd kinder like to ferret out
Why honest folks can ketch no trout.

In earlier days I had a wish
To Waltonize among the fish;
On lowery summer morns I rose
And donned my nifty rubber clothes
To mountain streams I slipped away,
But night fell, fishless, on my day,
While jest behind me that old scout,
Joe Nason got a string of trout.

I had a boughten bamboo pole,
While Joe had one I'm sure he stole;
I used some scented "acetate,"
While Joe jest spit upon his bait;
I had a fair repute to keep
While Joe was charged with stealing sheep
And yet, that sinful roustabout
Would always get his string of trout.

He lost a hand and then an eye,
But still could fish the county dry;
He never thought the times was tight
Unless the fish refused to bite;
I've set in church where I could look
And see him start for Purse's brook –
The worthless, wicked, lazy lout,
Yet somehow he could charm the trout.

hook, line & thinker

Except as stated, I can give
No reason why sech folks should live;
No man, because he fools the fish,
The ordered scheme of things should dish;
No man without a frock or friend,
Should stand the "moral world" on end,
And least of all, no worthless scout
Should eat my mess of speckled trout.[54]

Deception and dejection followed my initial anger. However, after an internal call to discipline my mood changed to reflection. The salmon hadn't budged an inch when I broke cover and sat on a rock beside the pool. There it was in full view not ten yards from me. I was trying to sort things out. Reviewing events, I concluded that I had made no mistakes: cover, flies, casting – everything according to the book. I then let the salmon's life pass before my mind's eye and pondered on the coincidence of our meeting. On the coincidence of any meeting of fisherman and fish. In theory the coincidence could be rationally explained by an infinite series of causal relations involving everything happening to the fish and to the fisherman. The problem is, of course, where to start or where to stop. Was our meeting caused by the fact that in the 19th century the fore-fore-fore ... father of that salmon there in the pool made it past the poachers? And how does this relate to my great-great-grandfather who fought and survived the battle of Austerlitz? Had he been killed I wouldn't be sitting here at this pool. Or would I? I was discovering causality and imponderables the hard way – and another thing crossed my mind: the salmon I was seeing all the time wasn't where I thought it was. The refraction of light always plays a trick – the fish is never there where you think it is. None of this was conclusive in any way, although it did greatly improve my state of mind and I actually started talking to the salmon. I was happy leaving the river that day. And besides, that salmon could have been one of the Salmons of Wisdom.[55]

Emerging from this are two interesting points. The first is that, contrary to what anti-anglers seem to think, it isn't fish galore all the time. On 9 May 2002 I counted eight boats on Lough Currane, Ireland. Each boat had two

---

54 http://www.ruralvermont.com
55 In Celtic mythology there are said to be five salmons of wisdom. If you catch one of them and eat it you'll be enlightened with all the world's wisdom. Incidentally, I've never caught a salmon on the River Avon.

anglers on it. Each angler presents his three-fly-cast at an average of three times per minute for between five and six hours. So that way the fish had 47,250 opportunities to take. None of them did. The second point is the element of "choice". It's an imponderable in the fishing equation. This is not the case in hunting. The moment the crosshairs are on target there is no more escape unless the hunter wills it so. In the case of the fisherman it's completely different: you can see the worm dangling in front of the fish or the fly floating above it. You can see the fish looking at it. There is, however, nothing but nothing you can do to hook that fish even if you want to. The angler can't deliberate like the hunter can. The relationship between fisherman and fish is more complex than de Leeuw and other anti-anglers suggest. Their accounts of what is happening in fishing, and not only on that score, are deficient.

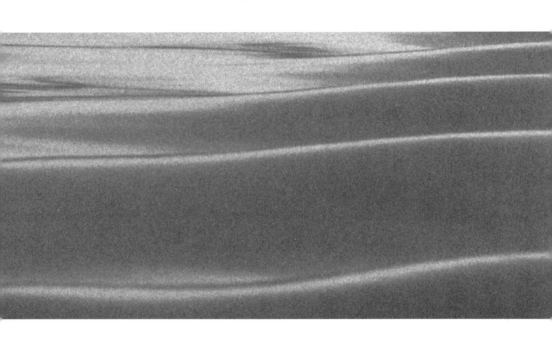

The holy gene

Evolution, as we have seen, is broadly speaking the theory that all present forms of life have developed from earlier forms. For most people there is no room for God in the process. In a paragraph discussing the theory of evolution Singer states:

> With the eventual acceptance of Darwin's theory we reach a modern understanding of nature, one which has since then changed in detail rather than the fundamentals. Only those who prefer religious faith to beliefs based on reasoning and evidence can still maintain that the human species is the special darling of the entire universe, or that other animals were created to provide us with food, or that we have divine authority over them, and divine permission to kill them.[56]

Juxtaposing "religious faith" and "beliefs based on reasoning" is a superb rhetorical move. But what does it mean apart from a gibe at religion? Is he saying that religious faith and science are mutually exclusive? Is he saying that it is impossible to be Christian and vegetarian? Or is it simply a vacuous remark? Whatever, he appears to suggest that "beliefs based on reasoning" are somehow superior from a moral, methodological and philosophical point of view. Regan makes a similar point in a dictatorial chapter entitled "Some ways not to answer moral questions"[57]:

> Most people who think there is a moral authority think that this being is not an ordinary person but a god. This causes problems immediately. Whether there is a god (or gods) is a very controversial question, and to rest questions of right and wrong on what an alleged god says (or the gods say) is already to base morality on an intellectually unsettled foundation.[58]

Discarding God and religion in this offhand manner shows a singular lack of willingness to seriously consider and appreciate the role of culture, tradition, the common wisdom of mankind and conscience. There is nothing

56 Peter Singer, *Animal Liberation*, Avon Books, New York (1991), p.206–207.
57 Tom Regan, *The Case for Animal Rights*, University of California Press, Berkeley and Los Angeles CA (1985), p.122.
58 Ibid., p.125.

intellectually unsettled about God, religion and ethics! How could there be? This is just a statement of a preconceived idea. On the contrary, it is flashy secular ethics that looks distinctly wobbly standing as it often does on the basis of subjectivism and on the fashionable free-for-all, anything-goes attitude. And just for the record: The myth of the enmity between science and Christian religion is still nurtured by those who would like it to be that way. The case of Galileo, probably the most often cited example of the church's negative stance on science, shows how little the sworn enemies of Christianity care about differentiating. In point of fact Galileo wasn't brought down by the cardinals but by his fellow academics.[59]

To the chagrin of moral philosophers there is no such dynamic in the history of ethics as there is in the history of science. In terms of changing the world, the pace of theory, discovery and invention in science has, since Greco-Roman times, accelerated to a breathtaking speed. Even the most cursory of glances at the last 150 years reveals that in all fields of natural philosophy and applied science, the horizon of knowledge and know-how has dramatically expanded. From galvanism to the laptop computer and from greenheart to carbon fibre rods – the improvements within a few generations have been stupendous.

In stark contrast, moral philosophy has advanced, if at all, almost imperceptibly. From pre-Socratic philosophers to the present time, the moral precepts (if any) discovered by moral philosophers resemble each other remarkably. The differences are primarily of emphasis. The Ten Commandments as a guideline could probably be accepted by most moral philosophers. That is no surprise either because in man's historical phase (the period of written documents)[60] his nature or basic condition in the sense of his needs and desires etc. hasn't changed at all. And as long as the rational and emotional framework remains more or less the same, the same conclusions more or less will be drawn in the moral domain as far as humans are concerned.

Where moral philosophy has progressed is on the output side. The degree of sophistication and volume is stunning. This doesn't apply just to

59 See: http://www.bbc.co.uk/history/historic_figures/galilei_galileo.shtml and
http://www.probe.org/docs/modmyths.html
The science of fly fishing owes a lot to the clergy. A case in point is the Canon William Greenwell of
Durham. See http://www.flyfishinghistory.com/greenwells_glory.htm
60 Written evidence of fly fishing goes back to the first century AD. See *The Fly* by Andrew Herd,
The Medlar Press Ltd, Ellesmere, England (2001), pp.22-23.

moral philosophy but to the other human sciences like psychology and sociology. Partly this is certainly due to the "publish or perish" blackmail trap in which university teachers are caught. Does a good teacher need to be a prolific writer? And does a prolific writer automatically make a good teacher? The reason I mention this is simply that a lot of writing about animal rights, all of which implies the end of angling, is not necessarily guided by noble motives and a pure scientific or philosophical interest in expanding the frontiers of knowledge, let alone the search for wisdom. There is a lot of occupational therapy here. The effects of that therapy will be felt once the ideas of animal rights have taken root in another generation or two of students, who will automatically be anti-anglers and anti-hunters. At a given moment in the not-too-distant future it might be simply taken for granted that angling is a bad thing – the foundations for such a state of affairs are laid. Every unchallenged pro-animal-rights paper is a contribution to that "cruelty-free" society in which angling and hunting certainly have no place.

Religion is here to stay. And God has a place in this world. Edward O. Wilson, although in purely functional terms, also thinks so:

> The predisposition to religious belief is the most complex and powerful force in the human mind and in all probability an ineradicable part of human nature.[61]

Of course, Wilson would love to replace contemporary religion with something more enlightened like "scientific materialism". Here is what he has in mind:

> I am suggesting a modification of scientific humanism through the recognition that the mental processes of religious belief – consecration of personal and group identity, attention to charismatic leaders, mythopoeism, and others – represent programmed predispositions whose self-sufficient components were incorporated into the neural apparatus of the brain by thousands of generations of genetic evolution. As such they are powerful, ineradicable, and at the center of human social existence. They are also structured to a degree not previously appreciated by philosophers. I suggest further that scientific materialism must

61 Edward O. Wilson, *On Human Nature*, Harvard University Press (2001), p.169.

*accommodate them on two levels: as a scientific puzzle of great
complexity and interest, and as a source of energies that can be shifted in
new directions when scientific materialism itself is accepted as the more
powerful mythology.*[62]

Who is going to answer your prayers at the riverside and elsewhere?
The Holy Gene maybe?

Predictably it's going to be a bumpy ride to scientific materialism unless
you go in for a bit of positive eugenics, nudging our mammalian nature in a
more rational and materialist direction. Eugenics is an idea that keeps
popping up regularly in the discussion about evolution and animal rights.
Eugenics tries to change the genetic make-up of humans in a way which
produces the traits the "eugeneers" want it to have. Negative eugenics is the
idea of actively preventing people from reproducing. In its "milder" forms it
means the following:

*In May 1927, Oliver Wendell Holmes, writing for the majority of the U.S.
Supreme Court, upheld involuntary sterilization of the feeble minded,
concluding: 'It is better for all the world, if instead of waiting to execute
degenerative offspring for crime, or to let them starve for their imbecility,
society can prevent those who are manifestly unfit from continuing their
kind. The principle that sustains compulsory vaccination is broad enough
to cover cutting the Fallopian tubes.'*
*The Supreme Court's decision to uphold the Virginia law accelerated the
pace of legislation: as was the case before World War I [when] a small
group of activists from influential quarters persuaded scientifically
unsophisticated legislators that sterilization was necessary, humane and
just.*[63]

I chose this example because of the "small group of activists from
influential quarters". Small and influential is also the appropriate description
of the animal rights elites, whose doctrines find their way into influential
homes via the five-star universities. A bit of whispering in a Prime Minister's
or President's ear from influential quarters outweighs many good arguments
and grievances.

---

62 Ibid., pp.206–207.
63 Philip R. Reilly, *Contemporary Issues in Bioethics*, ed. Tom L. Beauchamp and LeRoy Walters,
Wadsworth Publishing Company (1999), p.521.

Positive eugenics is the approach whereby you encourage able and healthy people to have more children in order to improve the overall quality of the human stock, so to speak. Today with genetic manipulation seemingly within reach, the idea is that you actually modify the genetic code. In this way parents (or the government, or big corporations etc.) can go to the genetic designer and shop for a child with blue eyes – think of it as ordering a new car. First you decide on the model, male or female. Then you think about the colour, then the size – there might even be catalogues with pictures of what the product will look like at the various stages between year one and 99. That is, if human beings will be allowed to get as old as that. The expiry date will be defined by the bio-authorities. A money-back guarantee surely wouldn't be a problem and certainly credit can be arranged... and so on. Fun really, isn't it? Anyway it doesn't end there. The following passage from a fairly intriguing website makes interesting reading and gives you an idea of what's in the minds of some animal rights activists:

> ... within the next hundred years or so, and possibly sooner, biotechnology can be used to stop the animal holocaust. It will enable the human species cost-effectively to mass-produce edible cellular protein, and indeed all forms of food, of a flavour and texture indistinguishable from, or tastier than, the sanitised animal products we now eat. As our palates become satisfied by other means, the moral arguments for animal rights will start to seem overwhelmingly compelling. The Western(ised) planetary elite will finally start to award sentient fellow creatures we torture and kill a moral status akin to human infants and toddlers. Veganism, though not quite in the contemporary sense, will become the norm. And the humblest snack will be more delicious than the ambrosial food of the gods ... "[64]

We still will need toilets but by reducing the human being to a single cell into which all humanness is packed, this problem can easily be overcome. Animals then will, out of gratitude for their liberation, look after those single-cell awarenesses. The point about all this is to illustrate what sort of multi-faceted unholy alliance anglers face. All or part of these seemingly disparate schools of thought will at a given time unite in support of one cause or another like the abolition of hunting and fishing. When the campaign is over they all go happily home riding their own particular hobbyhorse again.

64 http://www.paradise-engineering.com/heav24.htm

For our present discussion it is interesting to note that in Singer's and Regan's usage, "evolution" appears as a neat self-evident package on the basis of which philosophical arguments can be developed. Religion and God complicate things unnecessarily and don't feature in the animal rightists' philosophical inventory. Wilson, a scientist, recognises the importance of religion as a decisive factor in the evolutionary equation. God and religion have their place in the human world. This simple but vital fact is thrown out of the window by Regan and Singer because it doesn't fit their case. Or they don't care either way because in the end they replace one dogma with another and God's part is taken by their modest selves. Personally I would rather have God.

The really disconcerting trait is the nonchalance in presenting as hard, uncontested theory or fact – in this case evolution – what in reality is an ongoing scientific concern. Religion is not an ephemeral entity in human life. If you conceptually throw it out just like that, it's rather like saying that the Cambrian was of zero importance in the history of evolution.[65] On the other hand it is at the philosopher's discretion to ignore or to decide what is relevant for the case he is making. If religion is seen by Regan, Singer and others as the prime obstacle to the enlightenment of mankind then, yes, they're perfectly entitled to exclude it from consideration in their constructs. For understanding animal rights supporters in general you must be aware that they discuss religion in the same way as other areas (evolution, slavery, fairy tales, pain in fish) very skilfully, with well-informed distortion.

Christianity is the cement of Western culture. What Singer means when he points his finger at Christians, which he frequently does, is that Christian institutions and the doctrines they hold prevent man from understanding the real story of the universe and, worse, prevent him from seeing the truth about animals. Singer, Regan and many others are living proof that Christianity did not and cannot exert a stifling influence on science and philosophy.

"Beliefs based on reasoning" and "intellectually settled foundation": there's a convincing neatness to these phrases which makes you instinctively nod. But what do they actually mean? They mean that the champions of

65 The Cambrian is the period in the earth's history when many of the major groups of animals first appeared in the fossil records.

animal rights have faith in their logical methods and that the conclusions they arrive at are in a way objective:

I believe that the case for Animal Liberation is logically cogent, and cannot be refuted.[66]

Even if this were so, it leaves the question open as to why "logically cogent" should in any way be binding in the sense that you or I should give up fishing. Logically cogent does not necessarily mean that whatever is said corresponds to anything at all in the real world. What if the reasoning has gone wrong somewhere? There's no lack of recent historical events where "logically cogent" views of the world have gone awfully awry. Apart from that: what if the basic facts are wrong? [67]

My cousin Theresa is a most extraordinary woman. Nothing short of a monument could express my admiration for her. Blessed with wisdom, foresight, selflessness and consideration she married Max. Max, thank God, isn't interested in fishing and happens to own the fishing rights for three quarters of a mile of one of continental Europe's most beautiful trout waters. That stretch of water is open only for me. None of my relatives fishes. I can confidently assure all who dream of such bliss that reality is infinitely preferable to imagination.

So every year since Theresa's coup I go fishing there for a week or two. Towards the end of my stay I invite my numerous relatives for a dinner party at the local hotel where I stay (the hotel owns the adjacent stretch of that water). The chef there knows his business: nowhere else is the *truite meunière* of such classical perfection. The dash of Worcester sauce makes all the difference – but we leave that for some other time. Last year my relatives turned out in force. There were more than twenty people and practically all of them ordered my recently caught trout of which I said there were enough because the fishing had been good the last few days. I wasn't so sure about the Chablis but in the end there was enough. The party was a great success. Smiling and happy faces all round. My fishing skills were praised and I was basking in my piscatorial success. My reputation would rise to almost

---

66 Peter Singer, op.cit., p.244.
67 Facts are never "logically isolated from some kind of 'evaluating'" a point easily overlooked. You don't need to be a sceptic to appreciate this. See Mary Midgley, *Beast and Man*, Routledge, London (1998), p.178. On the other hand it is well to remember that there must be some sort of hard facts as the basis of discourse. Otherwise life and science aren't possible. The one that got away is a hard and bitter fact.

indecent heights. Deservedly so, I thought before Morpheus took me to his kingdom, because in my self-assessment my fishing had been tactically impeccable. My flies, which weren't in line with local wisdom, proved to be well tied and successful – so I had every reason to feel perfectly happy.

A couple of days later when it was time to say goodbye and to pay, I noticed an unusual item on the bill. "Trout" it said there. I asked, a bit perplexed what exactly was meant by "trout". The answer brought me down to earth. The trout I had supplied would have been enough for just half the guests. So the chef took the liberty of stretching my trout, so to speak. Apart from a well-developed capacity for self-delusion it just shows that you can't be careful enough about facts. If my relatives read this, which they most likely will, I'll have to rebuild my piscatorial reputation. Hard work but I won't flinch from the task – I am ready to face the challenge. In fact it will be a great pleasure.

Drawing lines

It seems somehow in the nature of Regan's and Singer's ideas and arguments that they really invite extensions, modifications and speculations beyond their declared boundaries. The line in Singer's case seems at first sight a rather clear one:

> To have interests, in a strict, nonmetaphorical sense, a being must be capable of suffering or experiencing pleasure... the problem of drawing the line is the problem of deciding when we are justified in assuming that a being is incapable of suffering.[68]

As Singer himself points out, the picture gets more and more blurred as we go down the evolutionary scale. In principle it could probably be said of all sentient beings that they can suffer. An excellent example of the inbuilt extendability beyond sentience is an article entitled "Respect for Life: Counting What Singer Finds of No Account". The author, Holmes Rolston III, shows that the frontiers can be pushed still further. The capacity to suffer, according to Singer, defines where moral value is, where interests lie and where consideration is due. Rolston III takes up the case for trees, plants and other insentient life and observes that

> We agree with Singer that there is no feeling in such an organism [a plant], but it does not follow that humans cannot or ought not to develop 'a feeling for the organism'.[69]

All it takes is a few words and literally everything is moved within range of moral consideration. Intended or not, in daily life this kind of philosophising leads some people, for example, to tree hugging. Tree hugging is perfectly okay with me. I talk to salmon, other people hug trees. No problem? Far from it.

Mushroom stalking is as engulfing as fishing. The other day I was prowling one of my favourite haunts: a lonely, forbidding wood. Very few

---

68 Peter Singer, op.cit., p.171.
69 Editor Dale Jamieson, *Singer and His Critics*, Blackwell Publishers, Oxford (1999), p.254. My brackets. My mother-in-law would fully agree with Rolston III. She talks to her plants and vegetables with stunning results. And then she slaughters them.

people venture into it. There I was, my wicker basket three quarters full of treasures such as ceps and chanterelles when I heard a faint rhythmic chant. Knowing that wood like the back of my hand I knew it could only come from a hollow a bit further on. Always eager for a chat with goblins or fairies I approached the scene. There were half a dozen people clad in colourful patchwork garments hugging trees and singing to them. I felt so embarrassed – it was like in one of those reality TV shows where people confess to something or other and then burst into tears. It is so unspeakably embarrassing I can't bear it. I have to switch off the telly. I cursed myself for having been curious – but wouldn't you have been curious too? Anyway it was too late to steal away and to bring matters up to a head, one of the group (a young woman in her twenties) approached me in her flowing robe, bare foot. I bid her a good day and got a harsh "What are you doing here?" in return. Still embarrassed I meekly pointed to the wicker basket. Maybe she thought that she was a cep (more likely a witch's egg) in one of her former lives – whatever, she obviously disapproved of what she saw. She mumbled something about damage and the environment and then asked me to go away because I would disturb them. I happily obliged.

Drawing the line is difficult. Take pain: what's the situation with mussels, for example? Singer isn't a hundred percent certain but the benefit of the doubt solves this problem easily: no mussels on your plate. The most general descriptions like "highly developed sensory organs" and "responses to certain stimuli immediate and vigorous"[70] are used to assert the potential capacity of prawns and shrimps to feel pain. How vigorous is significant? Not being a zoologist but all the same having a lively interest in tardigrades[71] I could also confidently say about them that "their sensory organs" apparently are highly developed and that their responses to certain stimuli are immediate and vigorous. And for good measure I might also add that they seem to know very well what they're doing. They move purposefully about and display a sense of the future. A very acute one because:

when the going gets tough, the tardigrade simply takes a nap until times are better ... once the hostile foe or unpleasant environment has passed, the tardigrade awakes as from a pleasant dream ready again to face the challenges of a new day.[72]

70 Peter Singer, op.cit., p.172
71 There's a lovely website on the subject: the "Tardigrade Appreciation Headquarters", http://q7.com/~vvv.tardigrade
Remember: the tardigrade is an important microscopic member of pond life society.
72 Quoted from the above mentioned website.

Future research methods will be even more sophisticated than today's. There will be more data available – with the flood of data the complexity will grow, social and sexual behaviour of tardigrades will be recorded and interpreted. And the more complex and beautiful tardigrades become, the more their humanness transpires. In short they're absolutely fascinating and amazing animals and their behaviour could be construed in a way to satisfy Regan's or Singer's criteria. Especially if some chemical substance of significance, relating tardigrades to human beings, is discovered. This shouldn't be too difficult because all life branched out from the same primaeval soup.

Why draw lines in the first place? Why go to all the trouble of determining which creatures have awareness and can feel pain and suffering? The principal reason is that Regan and Singer don't want to end up in an ethical position like that of Albert Schweitzer or that of Jainism[73]. According to Schweitzer and Jainism, compassion embraces all living beings, including plants, of course. If you snap a blade of grass and put it in your mouth, as you sometimes do for no particular reason, you commit an act of unacceptable, wanton violence. The most dedicated followers of Jainism wear a cloth over nose and mouth in order to avoid killing little creatures in the air while breathing. As you would imagine, their diet is not simply vegan – Jainists even exclude roots and some fruits from their menu because of the life in them.

In contrast to Jainism, Singer and Regan don't show a concern for life itself; nor does their compassion (if indeed there is any) encompass all living beings. For their line-drawing exercise they are only interested in parts of life, that is, such life which suffers and has self-awareness. Only beings that

73 There's an excellent website on Albert Schweitzer: http://www.schweitzer.org/english/ase/aseleb.htm / You'll find biographical data and lots of source material. Here is Schweitzer's definition of ethics "Ethics consist in my experiencing the compulsion to show all will-to-live the same reverence as I do my own. A man is truly ethical only when he obeys the compulsion to help all life which he is able to assist, and shrinks from injuring anything that lives. If I save an insect from a puddle, life has devoted itself to live, and the division of life against itself has ended. Whenever my life devotes itself in any way to life, my finite will-to-live experiences union with infinite will in which all life is one." Albert Schweitzer is, in my view, in a completely different league from Regan and Singer. Albert Schweitzer was a truly great man with culture.

There are various sources on the Internet for Jainism: http://www.fas.harvard.edu / is very good. Just type in 'Jainism' in the search facility. Other sites giving you an impression are:
http://www.terapanth.com/impressions/solutions.htm
http://www.jainism.free-online.co.uk
http://www.cs.colostate.edu/~malaiya/jainhlinks.html
http://www.jainism.org

suffer and/or are self-aware qualify for equal consideration and/or rights. All other life is excluded yet it is life all the same. All life has a most vital interest in being and staying alive. Suffering and self-awareness are arbitrary criteria constructed to draw lines. Singer and Regan desperately need to draw lines in order to demarcate their position from that of Jainism. Drawing lines is the string that keeps their philosophical bundle together. As long as the strings hold, they stay in business. As Jainists, they would be out of it.

If you're an animal you don't need to worry about the line-drawing exercise. As a human being, especially as a baby, you wouldn't want to be at the receiving end of philosophies which put shrimps, rats and dogs on the same moral footing as your baby self. The Sun King of utilitarian logic is especially endearing in this respect – while being fussy about pain in shrimps, he has no qualms about infanticide. In a letter to the *New York Review of Books* Singer writes in an answer to a review of his *Practical Ethics*:

> *First, he [the reviewer] is broadly correct when he says that in my view the secret killing of a normal happy infant by parents unwilling to be burdened with its upbringing would be no greater moral wrong than that done by parents who abstain from conceiving a child for the same reasons.*[74]

The reason why many people still don't subscribe to such 'enlightened' views about infanticide and animal rights is, of course – once more – Christianity and its teachers and followers. The pet fiend of most animal rightists and liberators is a man called Thomas Aquinas. St. Thomas lived around 700 years ago and wrote the *Summa Theologiæ*, a summary of Christian belief and teaching. The *Summa Theologiæ* keeps inspiring and infuriating people. The reason why the animal rightists and liberators' pulse quickens is that they see St. Thomas's teachings not only as hopelessly anthropocentric and speciesist but to this very day as too influential. For Peter Singer, Aquinas' view that

> *through being cruel to animals one becomes cruel to human beings*[75]
> reveals

74 *The New York Review of Books* (August 14, 1980). Source://http.//www.nybooks.com/articles/7324/ My brackets.
75 *Catholic Encyclopedia.* http://www.newadvent.org/cathen
The Roman Stoic Seneca (c.3BC–AD65) who thought the same doesn't get any mention or stick from Singer. Seneca is a fellow vegetarian and early campaigner against cruelty of all kinds. See Jacqueline Amat, *Les Animaux Familiers Dans La Rome Antique*, Les Belles Lettres, Paris (2002), p.226.

the essence of speciesism.[76]

Speciesism is defined as:

> *a prejudice or attitude of bias in favour of the interests of members of one's own species and against those of members of other species.*[77]

Time and again we're told in *Animal Liberation* that equal consideration for all suffering animals is the heart of anti-speciesism. Cruelty in fact is a sideshow in *Animal Liberation* for the simple reason that it isn't Singer's main concern. Yet suddenly out of the blue cruelty takes centre stage for no other apparent reason than to caricature Thomas Aquinas as the arch-speciesist.

All the same, according to Singer and his friends, speciesism is the root of all evil, and St. Thomas, i.e. Christianity, is the cause. Regardless of the "doubtful" source, the hint about there being a link between cruelty to animals and cruelty in human relations is happily taken up by some contemporary social scientists. The indiscriminate linking of "animal abuse" (of which fishing must logically be a part) and all sorts of social evils past and present is truly amazing. Slavery, oppression of women, juvenile delinquency, domestic violence – you name it and you're bound to find someone to tell you that this is all due to our warped relationship with animals, plants and nature in general. Animal abuse opens new intellectual opportunities – the streets are paved with it. All you need to do is to pick it up. An intellectual gold rush. The following example shows just how much you can put on your plate in one go – a gem, really. In the introduction to an essay titled: "Bringing Peace Home: A Feminist Philosophical Perspective on the Abuse of Women, Children, and Pet Animals", Carol J. Adams writes:

> *In this essay, I connect the sexual victimization of women, children, and pet animals with the violence manifest in a patriarchal culture. After discussing these connections, I demonstrate the importance of taking seriously these connections because of their implications for conceptual analysis, epistemology, and political, environmental, and applied philosophy. My goal is to broaden our understanding of issues relevant to creating peace and to provide some suggestions about what must be*

76 Peter Singer, op.cit., p.196.
77 Ibid., p.7.

included in any adequate feminist peace politics.[78]

That's quite a handful for a mercifully brief essay which starts with the words:

I have been a vegetarian since 1974.

If the last few paragraphs struck you as a bit far off fishing, don't be deceived. All these more or less refined theories aim at nothing less than a complete change of your way of life and by the same token the abolition of angling. The credos of the C.A.A. (Campaign for the Abolition of Angling) and A.L.F. (Animal Liberation Front) are simple derivatives from Regan's and Singer's philosophies. In fact the A.L.F. advertises Peter Singer's book *Animal Liberation*. On that very same page you find a blunt declaration of A.L.F.'s faith in violence:

The Animal Liberation Front (A.L.F.) carries out direct action against animal abuse in the form of rescuing animals and causing financial loss to animal exploiters, usually through damage and destruction of property.[79]

They mean business. Bombing and arson are in their repertoire which also comprises supremely inane activities such as liberating minks or just plain breaking and entering and so on. If you now think that this is just a crackpot minority group best ignored, you would be right if it were just that group. Together with literally thousands of other organisations lobbying legally for animal rights they form a force not to be ignored. The A.L.F.'s soldiers are recruited from militant vegetarians and vegans:

Any group of people who are vegetarians or vegans and who carry out actions according to A.L.F. guidelines have the right to regard themselves as part of the A.L.F.[80]

The key concern linking all the animal rights groups is the cruel treatment of animals by humans. Alleged fishing cruelty makes excellent propaganda:

78 *Cruelty to Animals and Interpersonal Violence*, Edited by Randall Lockwood and Frank R. Ascione, Purdue University Press, West Lafayette, Indiana (1998), p.318.
79 http://www.hedweb.com/alffaq.htm
80 Ibid.

Surely it is only because fish do not yelp or whimper in a way that we can hear that otherwise decent people can think it a pleasant way of spending an afternoon to sit by the water dangling a hook while previously caught fish die slowly beside them.[81]

This is superb rhetoric and from here it's only a step to:

Imagine reaching for an apple on a tree and having your hand suddenly impaled by a metal hook that drags you – the whole of your weight pulling on that one hand – out of the air and into an atmosphere in which you cannot breathe. This is what fish – who have well-developed pain receptors – experience when they are hooked.[82]

Implementation of animal rights means the end of fishing. Don't be lulled into thinking that ethics is of no importance to angling! Your angling stands or falls with it – fish and think!

81 Peter Singer, op.cit., p.172.
82 http://www.nofishing.net/sport.html

Chapter 4

SHORT CUT

Cruelty is defined by pain, distress and a will to (unnecessarily) inflict them. The Utrecht report is the most cited study by anti-anglers. It describes in detail what happens when a fish (carp) is hooked. The Utrecht study concludes that a hooked fish doesn't experience pain but fear. This is very fishy: how can it experience fear if it doesn't feel pain? Whether pain or fear, fish are not human beings with scales and fins. Fish experience is not human experience!

If it is said that fish pain is human pain but just further down the scale, there would have to be corresponding to pain also pleasure. This can be positively excluded because the fish brain is not organised like the human brain. Human pain involves an emotional dimension which is absent in fish. Qualitatively and quantitatively, human experience and fish experience are absolutely not the same. The situation can be summed up as follows:

1) The fish brain is not a miniaturised human brain. Or the other way round: a human brain is not an enlarged fish brain.
2) Fish experience is not human experience. Fish pain is not human pain.
3) Pain in the human sense doesn't mean anything to fish.
4) Fish lack the psychological or emotional dimension.
5) Fish "pain" is response to stimuli.
6) Fish response is not pain. Fish don't suffer.
7) No pain, no suffering, no cruelty.

It is said by anti-anglers that the enjoyment of angling consists in inflicting pain and suffering on fish. You can dismiss the case because if there is no pain and suffering how can there be enjoyment in inflicting it?

The object of fishing is to catch fish, not to torture them. And as for cruel anglers, how about cruel cat owners? In the following lines from the anti-angling philosopher, Dionys de Leeuw, I have simply added the italics to demonstrate the absurd notion of the cruel angler:

*The enjoyment of catching fish **(keeping a cat)** for sport **(for pleasure)** – consists of purposely inflicting fear, pain and suffering on fish **(birds)** by forcing them to violently express their interest to stay alive.*[93]

Cruelty in angling is merely a means to an end. Anti-anglers are not interested in fish – societal change is what they have in mind. As far as cruelty in angling is concerned, anglers have for far too long put up patiently with the charge. From now on the onus of proof is on the anti-anglers!

The bull

The components of cruelty are pain, distress and a will to inflict them. Distress by itself is not necessarily painful – but that is already a distinction leading into subtleties. Plain pain must be the basic interest because pain is the *sine qua non* of cruelty. No pain, no cruelty. No cruelty, no moral arguments against fishing. It's as simple as that.

Hooking and landing a fish are vital parts of any fishing: that first pull, the moment you realise a fish has taken is thrilling and so is playing and landing it. This is part of the experience and part of the pleasure. The object of fishing is to catch fish. Note the words here: the object is to catch fish – not, for example, to torture them or to mutilate them.

What happens in the process of a fish being caught? Although it's a while since the Utrecht report (1988)[83], I use it as the basis for my answer. The reason is simply that all anti-anglers refer either to the RSPCA-sponsored Medway[84] report or the Utrecht study or both. The more recent Utrecht study gets down to the nitty-gritty and this is what it says about the hooking experience:

Upon being hooked the fish make some rapid darts (1), and subsequently, while swimming freely on the slackened line, show spit (2) and shake head (3). Some carp resumed feeding only a few minutes later while swimming around with the slackened line. Reactions similar to responses (2) and (3) are also shown by a non-hooked fish when it gets unwanted material in its mouth while ventilating or taking food. The fish in play show behaviour designed as flee (4), spit gas (5), sink (6) and lie (7)85

One conclusion drawn from these observations is:

… we assume that reactions 4–7 of the hooked fish in play are indicative of fear, and not of pain.[86]

83 Prof. Dr. F.J. Verheijen and Dr. R.J.A. Buwalda, "Do pain and fear make a hooked carp suffer?" (1988), http://pisces.enviroweb.org/carpfear.html
84 http://www.pisces.demon.co.uk/factshe2.html
85 Ibid.
86 Ibid. Fear is yet another story which is not at the core of the cruelty charge.

Prick up your ears: no pain but fear! How can they fear if they don't even feel pain? Fear is a highly complex state involving psychological dimensions way above feeling pain. If the conclusion shows one thing for certain then it is the fact that you can't simply graft the human experience on fish. Little does it matter to anti-anglers: in the same way as everybody is happily babbling about evolution, everybody is seriously pretending that it is crystal clear what pain and suffering are!

If we look at the whole line-drawing business (especially Singer's) under the aspect of the blurred meaning of pain or the capacity to suffer, some interesting questions arise. Singer mentions oysters, to which we should give the benefit of the doubt (he isn't certain but assumes they do feel pain). Have oysters feelings? Do centipedes get jealous? Why do cockroaches always look so depressed? The cockroach is no joke. If the headline:

Cockroach Capable of Feeling Pain, Says Study[87]

corresponds to reality, why shouldn't it be capable of being depressed? In the article with the aforementioned headline you also learn that:

The discovery that slugs, snails and flies feel pain could change forever the way human beings treat the rest of the animal kingdom...[88]

and in the same item Prof. D. Broom reports on studies which show that cattle can react emotionally. And bulls have their moods too – as every angler knows only to well.

So, what can positively be said about pain in fish? The first fact is that fish have not the same pain experience as human beings do – if they had, they would be human beings with scales and flippers. This seems obvious but it obviously isn't to some. Fish pain is not human pain. Fish "suffering" is not human suffering. To the fish, pain as we understand it doesn't mean much – for all we know probably nothing at all.

Anti-anglers will ignore this and argue that the presence of specific pain pathways signifies that pain is felt all the same, but further down the

87 http://www.telegraph.co.uk / issue 1812 / Thursday 11 May 2000. Vanity, funds and fame are often the source of sensational new discoveries in science. The case of the German physicist Jan Hendrik Schön is a beautiful case in point. See: http://physicsweb.org/article/world/15/11/2
88 Ibid.

scale. If this were so, how far down the scale? Is the scale the same for lamprey, guppy and pike? And at which point of the pain scale, in an intelligibly comparative sense (if that is possible in the first place), does it cease to be pain? It's that drawing-the-line business all over again. The arbitrariness here gets into the picture via completely muddy concepts about the nature of pain.

It is more accurate to look at the situation in terms of stimulus and response. Stimulus/response expresses the factual situation of what happens more adequately than the pain/pleasure pair. Response brings out the fact that pain in fish is a different experience from pain in man. The crucial difference between pain in human beings and pain in fish is the emotional dimension. Suffering in the sense, for example, that the fish is tormented by the injustice done to it (its rights being violated, suffering inflicted) by the angler is non-existent. Fish lack the emotional dimension of the pain experience and just as absent are intelligence and psychological complexity in the human sense.[89] Fish do not feel pain or experience suffering as humans do, just as a cockroach is not a human in disguise. "Pain" and "suffering" are misnomers in the first place and the source of a lot of confusion. The same goes for pleasure and pain. It was recently discovered that

areas of the (human) brain that respond to feelings of pleasure also react to the sensation of pain.[90]

This is not the case in the fish brain and emphasises the point of pain in fish not being the same as in man because the fish brain is not organised that way. If it were human pain that fish feel, they would have to have the same brain layout. A fish brain is not a miniaturised human brain – if it were, a human brain would be an enlarged fish brain…

Fish and some philosophers do have, however, something in common: their sense of humour is non-existent. There are no jokes, no irony in the

89 The definition of pain in humans is not as easy as one would suspect. For the terminology of pain in humans see the website of the IASP, The International Association for the Study of Pain: http://www.halcyon.com/iasp/terms-p.html
The following explanation is also of interest: "There are two aspects to feeling pain: the actual physical sensation and your emotional response (the way it makes you feel)… The emotional part of pain is specific for each individual. The level of pain a person feels depends on a variety of factors, including their mood and what the pain means to them. This is why different people experience different levels of pain, even if they have the same physical condition." Source: http://www.napp.co.uk/pain/public/definmain.htm
90 http://news.bbc.co.uk / (my brackets)

animal kingdom[91] and this can also be said of many philosophical works. Nature, like some philosophers, can't afford not to be dead serious. If it had lapses of seriousness the consequences would be fatal. Just suppose a funny thought crossed a blackbird's mind as it was eagerly pulling out an earthworm. The blackbird would laugh and let go of the earthworm who, not believing his luck, would beat a hasty retreat. Then, with the blackbird laughing and its vigilance gone, a cat would pounce on it. There's no room for funny thoughts or downright jokes in a lot of philosophy either. Just imagine Kant telling a joke in his *Groundwork of the Metaphysics of Morals* – out of the question. The very title forbids it. Fish and man are not the same either in pleasure or in pain, though maybe fish and Kantians are, since neither show much emotion.

In order to be scrupulously fair and clearly understood I must emphasise that I am not saying that fish experience nothing when caught. The pain pathways (see Dr Morrow's explanation, page 99) and certain substances are indicators pointing to experiences of a sort – fish experiences, i.e. responses to stimuli without a psychological dimension. The fish experience differs qualitatively and quantitatively from human experience. There is really no point pretending that a fish or a shrimp is a human being!

Let's nevertheless stick to the assumed "pain" in order to look at it from yet another angle. Before man, there was no cruelty on earth and no animal rights and no need for animal liberation either. Only human beings can be cruel because they are moral agents. If we accept that there was no cruelty on earth before man, was there also no "pain" or "suffering" in the animal world, more specifically in the world of fish?

Of course there was from various sources, e.g. fish gulped down alive by birds, fish scarred by seals, fish stranded high and dry after a flood. What then is the difference between their "pain" and "suffering" then and now? None. Some of the sources of "pain" and "suffering" have changed. Somewhere along the line some predators disappeared from the scene, others entered it. Among the newcomers was the fisherman. And for all we know he might also be but an episode. The sum total of "suffering" remains the same.[92] "Suffer" the fish does whatever the source. It is of no care, consequence or comfort to it from what specific source it suffers. In the fish's equation, the angler is but a factor

91 Higher up in the evolutionary scale there is said to be laughter. See Mary Midgely, *Beast and Man,* Routledge, London (1998), p.228.
92 I am being for once hypothetical but not unreasonable: predator X disappears, the fish population increases which makes better living conditions for predator Y, the number of Y increases. And so on.

among many others. Anybody claiming that fish don't mind being torn apart and eaten by bears but strongly object to being caught and eaten by anglers somehow misses a point.

I also wonder how the people who claim that fish feel pain like human beings explain how such sensitive beings can survive in the first place in their environment. Predators apart, there are other sources of pain or discomfort for fish such as floods, droughts, fungus diseases and leeches. If in their harsh environment they could feel pain as human beings do, they would be long since gone. Extinct. Fish certainly don't experience cold like human beings nor the agony of deep open wounds as inflicted by cormorants, seals or other fish. An injury like that would cause a human being to faint with pain. The fish doesn't faint, it tries to and often does survive – with a human pain experience it wouldn't. Even scaled down human pain in fish doesn't make sense for the fish. Time and environment-wise, fish have lived a completely different experience. Fish have other things to learn than human beings. Not being a salmon and having other than an enlarged salmon brain, I don't have to learn how to find my home river. It just wouldn't make sense unless I am a salmon in disguise. It can't be emphasised enough and that's why I repeat it here again: fish pain isn't human pain! To present fish pain as identical or analogous to the human experience is more than distortion, it's downright dishonest.

Pain is at the core of every cruelty charge. In view of the apparent factual and speculative difficulties of drawing the line (in the Singerian sense) and the blatant misconceptions and misrepresentations of pain in fish, I wonder whether one should not ask a completely different question in the first place. Until now we have always assumed that the onus is on the anglers to show that fishing is not cruel. But shouldn't the question rather be: how can angling be cruel? Hasn't the anti-angler got a case to prove?

All anglers are cruel

Our point of departure was the conclusion of an article by A. Dionys de Leeuw in which he boldly asserts:

The enjoyment of catching fish for sport, in a large measure, consists of purposely inflicting fear, pain and suffering on fish by forcing them to violently express their interest to stay alive.[93]

Full blast, no holds barred. In order to fully appreciate the glorious vacuousness of this, take it at face value. You plan to go fishing. The last thing before you sleep is your resolution: tomorrow I am going to torture, abuse, stress and insult those bloody fish. The first thing you say to yourself in the morning is: I am looking forward to mutilating a few trout. I'll tear their ears off. You're cruelty personified. All fishermen are like that. None of them is interested in nature, wildlife, scenery, poetry, food, thought – they're all dumb oxen, murderous, bloodthirsty, cruel maniacs.

The idea of the cruel fisherman is eyewash. My neighbour manages an orphans home run by the Salvation Army. Apart from coping with a very demanding job, he and his family also engage in volunteer community work. They are frightfully virtuous. To describe a family like theirs as cruel seems ludicrous – no they don't go fishing, they keep a cat! The cat as the always-on-duty ornithologist in the family, causes a lot of suffering. However obliquely, by keeping the cat, my neighbours are cruel. They keep the cat for pleasure, and my fishing rod is their cat.

The enjoyment of catching fish (keeping a cat) *for sport* (for pleasure) – *consists of purposely inflicting fear, pain and suffering on fish* (birds) *by forcing them to violently express their interest to stay alive.*[94]

It's revealing that De Leeuw seems to think that the enjoyment could only consist of the infliction of suffering. Nonsense. Fishermen's dreams gyrate more around "An Angler's Wish" by Henry van Dyke:

---

93 A. Dionys de Leeuw, *Environmental Ethics,* "Contemplating the Interests of Fish: The Angler's Challenge", p.387.
94 Ibid. My brackets.

I

When tulips bloom in Union Square
And timid breaths of vernal air
Go wandering down the dusty town,
Like children lost in Vanity Fair.

When every long, unlovely row
Of westward house stands aglow
And leads the eyes toward sunset skies
Beyond the hills, where green trees grow -

Then weary seems the street parade,
And weary books, and weary trade:
I'm only wishing to go a-fishing;
For this the month of May was made.

II

I guess the pussy-willows now
Are creeping out on every bough
Along the brook; and robins look
For early worms behind the plough.

The thistle birds have changed their dun
For yellow coats, to match the sun;
And in the same array of flame
The dandelion show's begun.

The flocks of young anemones
Are dancing round the budding trees:
Who can help wishing to go a-fishing
In days as full of joy as these?

III

I think the meadow-lark's clear sound
Leaks upward slowly from the ground,
While on the wing the blue-birds ring
Their wedding bells to woods around.

The flirting chewink calls his dear
Behind the bush; and very near,
Where water flows, where green grass grows,
Song-sparrows gently sing, "Good cheer."

And, best of all, through twilight's calm
The hermit-thrush repeats his psalm.
How much I'm wishing to go a-fishing
In days so sweet with music's balm!

IV

'Tis not a proud desire of mine
I ask for nothing superfine;
No heavy weight, no salmon great,
To break the record – or my line:

Only a little idle stream,
Whose amber waters softly gleam,
Where I may wade, through woodland shade,
And cast the fly, and loaf, and dream:

Only a trout or two, to dart
From foaming pools, and try my art:
No more I'm wishing – old-fashioned fishing,
And just a day on Nature's heart.[95]

Fish, as Rupert Brooke expounds, see the matter in a slightly different light.

95 http:// www.bartleby.com

Heaven

FISH (fly-replete, in depth of June,
Dawdling away their wat'ry noon)
Ponder deep wisdom, dark or clear,
Each secret fishy hope or fear.
Fish say, they have their Stream and Pond;
But is there anything Beyond?
This life cannot be All, they swear,
For how unpleasant, if it were!
One may not doubt that, somehow, Good
Shall come of Water and of Mud;
And, sure, the reverent eye must see
A Purpose in Liquidity.
We darkly know, by Faith we cry,
The future is not Wholly Dry.
Mud unto mud!—Death eddies near—
Not here the appointed End, not here!
But somewhere, beyond Space and Time,
Is wetter water, slimier slime!
And there (they trust) there swimmeth One
Who swam ere rivers were begun,
Immense, of fishy form and mind,
Squamous, omnipotent, and kind;
And under that Almighty Fin,
The littlest fish may enter in.
Oh! never fly conceals a hook,
Fish say, in the Eternal Brook,
But more than mundane weeds are there,
And mud, celestially fair;
Fat caterpillars drift around,
And Paradisal grubs are found;
Unfading moths, immortal flies,
And the worm that never dies.
And in that Heaven of all their wish,
There shall be no more land, say fish.[96]

96 Rupert Brooke, *The Complete Poems*, AMS Press, New York (1977), p.132.

This leads to the final item. It's a point that comes in various guises:

The interest that anglers demonstrate in sport fishing is recreational and not a basic, or necessary, survival interest.[97]

Our man is definitely not a fisherman. How can angling not be a basic survival interest? Work or any other activity in daily life is but filling in the gaps between fishing sessions. Anyway, what is being said is the following: anglers are cruel and – worse – they're cruel for the wrong reasons. If a Seychellois fisherman fishes with lines festooned with dozens of hooks and hooks a fish, it "suffers" the same way as it does on my hook. Even more so because the Seychellois waits until there is a fish on every hook on his line before he pulls in. All the same the Seychellois subsistence fisher is regarded as less cruel[98] than I who fish for recreational reasons. It isn't really the fish or the interests of fish that are being discussed, but the angler. His thinking, his ideas, his way of life. The Seychellois fisherman poses an additional problem: he likes fishing. He takes pride in what he does and he looks on the day's catch with the pleasure of a job well done. Doesn't all the pleasure he gets out of his job make him really cruel too?

Where does all this leave the seemingly clear-cut concept of cruelty? Nowhere. De Leeuw and others really are in no position to launch charges of cruelty. It's the other way round: what is required of anti-anglers is positive proof that fish feel pain and experience suffering and that fishermen take pleasure in inflicting that condition on fish – if it can be inflicted in the first place.

---

97 A. Dionys de Leeuw, op.cit., p.377.
98 PETA (People for the Ethical Treatment of Animals): "Question: 'What about people who have to hunt to survive?' Answer: 'We have no quarrel with subsistence hunters and fishers who truly have no choice in order to survive. However in this day and age, meat, fur and leather are not a necessary part of survival for the vast majority of us.'" By implication the Seychellois should however also give up fishing. Living where he does he doesn't really need to fish. Theoretically. http://www.peta-online.org/fp/hunt.html

Homo sapiens sapiens: modern man

There is another important angle on cruelty: alleged cruelty in fishing or hunting is simply an attractive argument for animal rights activists – a means to an end. Fishermen and hunters can be presented as the embodiment of cruelty and as a major obstacle on the way to a "cruelty-free" society. "Cruelty-free" society ultimately is the goal of animal liberation. What man's place in nature is in such a society is far from clear. We can only guess from certain indications what a "cruelty-free" society means. Vegetarianism is one thing but the more daring visionaries wouldn't hesitate to use genetic engineering to remedy nature's wrongs such as the impossible situation of the antelope and the cheetah. The cheetah can't help himself from chasing and killing antelopes. There is a lot of "suffering" involved on the antelope's side. It is also that kind of "suffering" which one day will be overcome by a "cruelty-free" society.

Less obvious but still a problem for a "cruelty-free" society is, for example, birdsong. If you enjoy birdsong in spring, the delight you take originates in male birds desperately and aggressively trying to mark their territory and to attract mates. Isn't it a cruel pleasure originating as it does in the poor male birds' struggle? Are you morally entitled to enjoy birdsong? Shouldn't you rather be morally shaken to your very foundations and work towards the liberation of female birds from aggressive male behaviour?

That nature needs some mending doesn't necessarily follow from the philosophies of Singer and Regan. It might. The more radically inclined animal rightists are already concocting abstruse theories to do away with nature's unjust ways. Philosophically speaking, the radical fringe of the animal rights movement might not even have understood the theories of Singer and Regan yet for all practical purposes their reasons for action link directly to Singer and Regan.

Nature isn't all that different from what it was 2,500 years ago when Western philosophy got off the ground with the pre-Socratics[99]. After all,

99 The pre-Socratic philosophers like Thales or Heraclitus are thus called because they lived and taught before Socrates. Socrates is the key figure in the making of modern philosophy. His teachings inspired Plato and Aristotle who in turn influence to this day all philosophical discussions. See http://www.forthnet.gr/presocratics/indeng.htm and http://www.nd.edu/Departments/Maritain/etext/hop07.htm

2,500 years is a flicker in terms of earth history. Evolution is said to have started 3.5 billion years ago. The anatomically modern man appeared about 100,000 years ago. The breathtakingly short time it has taken man to get a seemingly dominant hold on the planet is truly amazing. Equally astounding is that man has been fishing for thousands of years and nobody noticed that it was cruel.[100]

The most important reason why nobody noticed is that it isn't cruel. The invention of cruelty was helped by the visual presence of anglers. In the past 50 years angling has grown into a popular sport. Millions and millions of anglers go fishing on a regular basis. Everybody is but a couple of handshakes away from somebody who fishes. The success of making hunting and by implication angling an issue is a great triumph for the animal rightists. Suddenly the shadow of suspicion falls on the friendly next-door neighbour who fishes: is he a fish torturer?

The other major contribution to the angling-is-cruel myth is the Bambi factor.

The 'Bambi complex', 'Bambi factor' and 'Bambi syndrome' are three terms used interchangeably for sentimental, sympathetic attitudes toward wildlife, especially deer.[101]

Bambi in particular is not to blame – it's the flood of humanised animals in books, animated cartoons and films. Just think of all the TV series since the Sixties such as *Fury*, *Lassie*, *Flipper*, *Mr. Ed* and all the Disney productions involving animals or all the "wildlife" films like *Free Willy* or all the cartoons like *Tom and Jerry*. These productions are by themselves really no problem. They're good entertainment – or are they?

Man was for thousands of years very close to the animal world. And had he not succeeded in creating a little distance between himself and the animals, we still might be very close – too close for comfort.

The typical mountain house was a shepherd's or herdsman's dwelling built for animals rather than for human beings. In 1574, Pierre Lescalopier,

---

100 I have tried to find out when the first specific cruelty charge was launched against angling. I haven't succeeded.
101 http://www.majbill.vt.edu/history/barrow/hist3144/readings/bambi.html. This is an absolutely brilliant article highlighting and explaining the problems Bambi generates.

when crossing the Bulgarian mountains, preferred to sleep 'under some
tree' than in the peasants' huts of beaten clay where beasts and humans
lived 'under one roof, and in such filth that we could not bear the
stench'[102]

Why choose this passage? First of all it's only 300 years ago. Secondly, at that time wildlife was rampant with bears, wolves, foxes, boars, eagles – the lot. Consider also that the region was sparsely populated and then imagine what the days and above all the nights were like. The solitude, the loneliness and the very real competition with wildlife. Man was literally one with nature. Comparisons quite naturally forced themselves into the minds of people: the sly old fox, the helpless lamb and, of course, the big bad wolf. Singer, as you would suspect also has something to say about wolves. With his usual sweeping confidence he asserts:

Not so long ago children were brought up on fairy tales in which animals,
especially wolves, were pictured as cunning enemies of man.[103]

Wolves and other animals in fairy tales were used metaphorically – yet animal rightists present them as part of the Christian conspiracy to maltreat animals. Fairy tales were not designed as propaganda against wolves or any other animal. Besides, there are also good wolves to be found in literature.[104] Fairy tales are another instance of the method of well-informed distortion employed by Peter Singer and other thinkers for the animal cause.

There were lots of things going on in the animal world which lend themselves to comparisons and it wasn't the age of sociobiology yet. Fairy tales and fables were made for vivid and popular ethical teaching and were handed down from one generation to the next. There was an oral tradition which today is lost because the stories can now be stored: in books, in films, on CDs and so on. In all ethical teaching you need the concepts of good and bad, right and wrong – in the fairy tales these concepts were represented by animals. Given the living conditions and first-hand experience people had of animals, it isn't surprising that the wolf was often cast for the baddie. The wolf back then in the Bulgarian mountains was probably not only perceived as threatening, but it was a real competitor or at least a nuisance in an

102 Fernand Braudel, *The Mediterranean World in the Age of Philip II*, Fontana (1978), p.42
103 Peter Singer, Peter Singer, *Animal Liberation*, Avon Books, New York (1991), p.214.
104 For example: Viktor Gazak, *Das Buch aus reinem Silber, Eine Märchenreise vom Amur bis zur Wolga*, mvs Verlag, Düsseldorf (1984). The fairy tale in question is: "Ivan-Zsarevitch und der graue Wolf", (Ivan Zsarevitch and the Grey Wolf).

economy where every single sheep mattered. So Singer is right to some degree but distorts the reasons why wolves were so depicted.

City and campus nature is cosseted. In that environment the nature of nature becomes more and more out of focus. In a cosy, clean climate – harmonised, balanced, liberated, respectful, temperate, considerate, unselfish, painfree, loving, caring, conflict-free, apolitical, just and well-brought-up omni-suburban world with vegetarian cats – there is no room for anything as downright archaic and prosaic as fishing. Or hunting. There is, however, a world between being cruel and simply outdated!

Emotional Bambi power amplified by animal rights propaganda is for real. In his brilliant, incisive and thoughtful article *Eating Bambi: Disney Comes to Dinner in Dixie* Gerald L. Smith, 'a hunter, hunting apologist, hunter safety instructor, and law enforcement associate', describes the conversion of a young student to the cause of animal rights:

One year in early winter, sometime after Thanksgiving, Dad had killed a deer and the processed meat had been brought home to the freezer. In the course of time, Mom had prepared a roast for dinner and all the family, including Ellen, had sat down to table. Ellen was about eight or nine years old at the time. The table conversation had had no particular direction until Ellen noticed that the meat tasted different from the family's customary beef and she had said so. Mom replied that it was not beef but venison. Ellen did not make the immediate connection. Mom explained: 'Venison is deer meat. Dad shot a deer at camp.' Ellen became quiet. Her brothers and father continued to eat and talk until one noticed that Ellen was silently crying. One brother called out, 'Look at Ellen; she's crying.' 'What's wrong honey?' the inevitable question; the inevitable Celtic reference to girls. Ellen was silent for a moment and never raised her eyes above her lap as she replied, 'Bambi. You ... killed Bambi.'

A little girl at the communion of the family table had just learned a hard lesson about the world and about her father and brothers. Not only did things die like the squirrel by the power pole in the back yard and the baby bird under the nest after the storm. She already knew these things. What she now learned was that some animals were killed and did not just die naturally, and they were killed and cut up and eaten by her Dad and Mom and brothers right in front of her, eaten by her not knowing what she was doing. It might have ended there in a deep and private resolution by Ellen

*not to eat deer meat ever again. Comforting or stern or wise words might
have been spoken to assuage her. Or there might have been a hug that
enfolded her again in the old order of things closer and truer than the family
table itself. But it did not end there. …*

*Ellen was sitting at the dinner table with tears falling from her cheeks. She
was not hugged or comforted or even just left alone. Brothers began to
taunt her, holding up their forks, sucking noisily at the juices. One let the
broth roll down his chin. They chanted together, 'Slurrp, slurrp. We're eating
Bambi. Munch. Munch. Munch. We're eating Bambi. Nanny, nanny, nanny.'
Her father laughed. Ellen never ate meat again. In the span of two minutes
a radical anti-hunter was created in a family of hunters. And she pursued
her cause with a fervor to match her father and her brothers' hunting
passion. Eventually, as she entered high school, she read anti-hunting
literature; she began to study Buddhism. She worked out a personal
philosophy of vegetarianism and a powerful agenda of opposition to the
beef industry, agri-business and sport hunting. But she was not a private
philosopher… She had good reasons and high motives. And as a teacher
and environmentalist, she would have an audience her father and brothers
would never be able to reach – or mend.* [105]

If as a fisherman you think that this doesn't concern you because it's
about hunting, you are mistaken. Hunting is different in many ways from
fishing but structurally the same arguments can be levelled against angling
as against hunting. If you're not convinced, think of the phenomenal
worldwide success of *The Rainbow Fish*,[106] a beautifully made children's
book about a little fish: an aquatic Bambi. What would you say if there was
a little girl asking you why you killed the Rainbow Fish?

Cruelty in fishing and hunting is not an argument about fish or deer. It's
about a conception of the world and an ideal of what society ought to be
("cruelty-free"). The main problem is that none of the prominent philosophers
or propagandists of animal rights can tell us in practical terms what they
would like society to be. Marxism was at least very precise on that. Animal
rights is not a homogeneous political programme. It's all very diffuse and
emotionally very appealing and that is part of its success because the fight for
animal rights, liberation and the environment offers a playground for
everybody.

105 http://sewanee.edu/gsmith/Texts/Hunting/EatingBambi.html
106 Marcus Pfister, *The Rainbow Fish*, North-South Books, New York (1992).

97

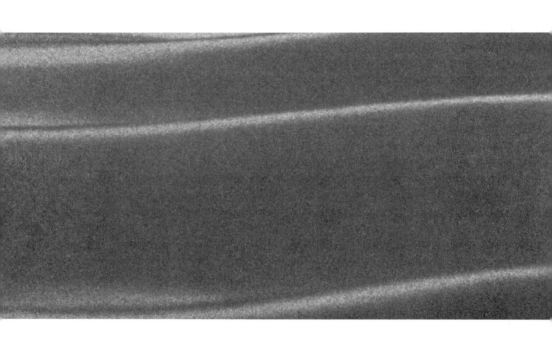

The conclusion

Back to the original question: "Can angling be cruel?" Pain and suffering are the core of the cruelty charge. A lot of water has flowed under the bridge since the Medway Report and the Utrecht study, so frequently cited by anti-anglers. Current scientific opinion backs up the common sense observation that a fish brain is not a scaled-down human brain.

Dr. Julie Morrow, Texas Tech University, USA :

Pain is transmitted by specific neural pathways and receptors for pain may be activated by mechanical, thermal or chemical stimuli. Fish possess these types of receptors in their skin. In humans, pain is sent to higher brain centers (prefrontal cortex) where it is perceived and the perception is associated with powerful emotional experience. Fish however, do not possess these well developed higher brain centers and thus they probably perceive a painful stimulus and react to it almost as a reflex. After the initial perception, they would not be bothered by the stimulus, similar to what occurs in humans who have had surgery to central brain regions to treat chronic pain.[107]

Dr. Mario Wullimann, University of Bremen, Germany:

The latest book on fish physiology doesn't even have the word pain in the index. Of course common sense tells you that it must be distressing for a fish to be hooked.[108]

Dr. Peter Fraser, Aberdeen University, Scotland:

There is unlikely to be controversy about there being specific pain pathways. What is more controversial is what the brain does with the signals. I for one would be reluctant to accept that fish feel pain as humans do.[109]

107 http://aquanic.org/publicat/state/il-in/faq/pain.htm
108 E-mail from Dr. Wullimann 15.03.2002.
109 E-mail from Dr. Fraser 07.01.2002.

Dr. James D. Rose, University of Wyoming, USA:

The facts about the neurological processes that generate pain make it highly unlikely that fish experience the emotional distress and suffering of pain. Thus the struggles of a fish don't signify suffering when the fish is seized in the talons of an osprey, when it's devoured while still alive by a Kodiak bear, or when it is caught by an angler. [110]

Prof. George Iwama, University of British Columbia, Canada:

Stress physiology, and how stress affects the immune system is my research interest. I work with fish. The issue you raise can never be unequivocally resolved. The relevant data are sparse. Even if we arrived at a point when all possible experiments had been conducted, and all such data were available, the conclusion to the question you pose, would be conjecture. It is simply the way it has to be about attributing our human experiences to non-human organisms. While this is clearly short of a satisfactory resolution, it is the clearest I can be on the subject. [111]

Before concluding, let's summarise the salient points of this chapter:

1. Cruelty is the deliberate causing of suffering.
   Human beings can be cruel to one another.
   Human beings can be cruel to animals if the latter are capable of suffering.

2. Animals can't be cruel.

3. The fish brain is not a scaled-down human brain.
   The human brain is not an enlarged fish brain.

4. *Conscious experience of fear, similar to pain, is a neurological impossibility for fish.* [112]
   Fish are not humans with scales and fins.

---

110 http://www.cotrout.org/do_fish_feel_pain.htm.
111 E-mail from Prof. Iwama 18.03.2002.
112 This chapter was written before I knew of Dr. James Rose's article "The Neurobehavioral Nature of Fishes and the Question of Awareness and Pain", Reviews in Fisheries Science, 10(1): 1-38 (2002) © CRC Press LLC. I was extremely pleased to learn that what at the time of writing was speculation for me has turned out to be scientific hard fact.

5. Fish experience is not human experience. Fish pain is not human pain.

6. Pain in the human sense doesn't mean anything to fish. Fish lack the psychological or emotional dimension.

7. Fish "pain" is a response to stimuli. Fish response is not pain. Fish don't suffer.

8. No pain, no suffering, no cruelty.

9. Conclusion: angling is not cruel.

To round off this chapter on cruelty here's some additional food for thought: manifest cruelty to sweet animals opens Disney-fied urban minds and purses. The poor seal, the poor whale, the poor rabbit, the poor cat, the poor bird: all animals with exposure potential are welcome material for animal rights propaganda. Fishing is said to be cruel for the reason that the fisherman inflicts pain and suffering. We have seen that this cannot be the case. For argument's sake, let's ignore that for the moment – the fisherman is thus held morally responsible for causing pain and suffering. Birds do feel pain and experience suffering – every animal rights supporter will agree to that. It would be very strange if he or she denied that birds suffer because if fish do, birds do. That being the case, why is it that we have never heard of a large scale campaign to abolish cat keeping? There are an estimated 100 million cats on the prowl in the United States, killing between 4 and 5 million of our feathered friends a day.[113] That's a fearsome lot of daily agony (not counting the toll in rodents, frogs and other small animal life; not counting suffering and pollution caused by the production of cat food) for which cat owners by pandering to such killers are at least obliquely responsible. Why should people keeping cats not be equally attacked for cruelty like hunters or fishermen? The reason why animal rights activists turn a blind eye to this situation is, of course, money: fund-raising. No organisation will dare to alienate millions of people who – in their self-assessment – love nature and animals. Keeping a cat can't be cruel whereas fishing and hunting must be cruel.

113 http://www.batnet.com/wildlife/education.html and http://whyfiles.org/urban_critter

"Cruelty-free" people who keep cats or dogs do have a problem inasmuch as cats and dogs are not vegetarians or vegans. The solution to this problem is simple:

The only truly ethical and non-hypocritical way to approach the no kill philosophy of carnivorous animals is to commit ourselves to converting these animals to true vegetarians (vegans).[114]

Well…

The other day I was fishing the lonely middle stretches of one of those magnificent Scottish east Highland rivers. Wild trout was on my mind. I was planning to fish right into the night, for that is when the big fellows start moving. I was therefore not unduly worried by the bright sky. On arrival at my likely spot, I sat on the crest of a little hill to wait and watch. That hillock separated the bend that the river was forming there. I couldn't see much upstream for the terrain was hiding the river but for the downstream scene this was the ideal vantage point. About a hundred yards downstream the river took its next turn and there was a fence demarcating the end of the Association water.

The shadows grew longer and a few golden-red fleecy clouds competed in colour density with a deep blue sky. So clear was the blue, you could see with the naked eye to the end of the universe. As the colours gradually faded out, the action started. A ripple here, a ripple there. As I spotted the first few trout moving I descended. I couldn't quite figure out what they were feeding on and so opted for a Greenwell's Glory. And a good choice it turned out to be. I missed a few but landed two nice, hard-fighting trout. These fish are incredibly strong for their size. The sun had now gone down but visibility was still good. So I had no trouble making out that there on the other side, about 20 yards from me at the neck of a little cascading stretch, something substantial was moving. I waited to verify. Darkness does play tricks on you. A branch stuck against the bank or in some stone can look in the current like a trout rising. But this was no branch, this was at least three pounds of

114 http//www.all-creatures.org/articles/petfood-nokill.html

beautiful trout. No doubt.

It was one of my good fishing days. I kept cool. I moved about unhurriedly, purposefully, and as the line flew out across the river, I already knew that the big fish would take me. Every angler experiences that sort of premonition. There is no explanation for it – you simply know what is going to happen. That cast was of such perfection that the Greenwell's Glory didn't land on the water. Like a prima ballerina it gently and gracefully set down on the points to begin a lively and seductive downstream dance. Big jaws didn't hesitate for a second. Splash and the action was on. The might of the pull triggered that sort of inner movie in which you can see yourself doing things in the past while being fully concentrated on what is happening in the present. It's the same when you drive off for a holiday, and an hour or so after you have left you ask yourself whether or not you have locked the front door. In this instance, tying the knot was the theme of the retro cinema. The knot held. The beauty was three and a half pounds and, after what seemed ages, it was safely landed and in the bag. Great joy overcame me and to this very day I remember every detail of that wonderful catch.

Also, to this very day, a cold shiver runs down my spine when I think of the terrible fright I got upon hearing a light squelching noise and turned around. There, on that hillock behind me, standing in threatening silence and darkness, were a dozen Highland cattle had presumably followed the action all along. Silhouetted against the still luminescent sky they looked like a proud band of Celtic warriors all set to charge down on me. In fact the biggest of them all, a hairy giant, the chieftain so to speak, set his mass in motion towards me while the others looked on stoically. While I hastily packed my gear, the bovine colossus paused for a minute as if to size me up. I chose to play it as cool as possible which was easier said than done. That fence now looked miles away. In fact it couldn't have been much more than fifty yards because the fishing had taken me downstream.

I started walking slowly, looking back every second or third step only to see with great dismay that the chieftain had obviously taken a keen interest in me. It followed at a slightly increased pace, closing the distance between its enormous horns and me. Consequently I went a bit faster but as in a nightmare, the bull came closer and closer and I moved in slow motion on the spot. But this time there was no waking up all in a sweat. This was for real and I could already feel the hot breath down my neck. I gave it all I had and behind me I could hear the pulse of my fate. I didn't stumble in the dark and with a great leap which would have done Gordon Banks proud, I landed on the other side of the fence. A close run thing if ever there was one. Still panting I looked back over the fence. The bull looked at me – at least I thought it looked because you can't really tell with Highland cattle. Then it shook its shaggy mass, gave a snort and sauntered back towards its fellow warriors, which were standing motionless on that hillock. Almost dark it might have been but as my pursuer turned I could see enough of her to realise that I had been mistaken all the way. Don't accept any bull!

Chapter 5

SHORT CUT

Vegetarianism is the application of a philosophical theory into everyday life. A word of caution though: not every vegetarian is necessarily an animal rights supporter. There are other meaty arguments about vegetarianism. Health is one of them. Some people simply feel that a vegetarian diet is better for them. Then there are the culinary objectors and a large group who, not surprisingly, simply feel uneasy about the way things are in the agri-business. There are also people who can't bear the thought of eating meat. All these people don't necessarily espouse full-blooded animal rights and their implications. The vegetarians and vegans that are the subject of this chapter are those that do, on the basis that:

the ultimate objective of the rights view is the total dissolution of the animal industry as we know it.[122]

Such is the intensity of some animal liberators' conviction that animals are like human beings that they take complete leave of their senses. The following statement is not the odd one out. Comparisons like it are rampant in animal rights propaganda:

Six million Jews died in concentration camps, but six million broiler chickens will die this year in slaughter houses.[123]

This monstrosity is beyond belief. Yet it is for real. The Holocaust, the attempt to exterminate a human culture, is attributed the same status as the slaughtering of broiler chickens in one year. In other words the death of a chicken equals a human victim – there is no difference between them. Here you have Singerian "equal consideration" in its purest form, the true face of Animal Liberation.

Animal rights vegetarians don't tire of pointing out who is responsible for all the past and present suffering in the animal kingdom. Yes, you're right: Christianity and Western culture. And when it comes to slandering them, all means seem to be justified. The most insidious tactic is that of well-informed distortion of historical fact or circumstance. Christianity is, among many other things, said to be responsible for an

incalculable sum of cruelty [131]

to animals. Has Christianity invented the maltreatment of animals? Was there no cruelty to animals before Christianity? Animal rightists don't even look for an answer. It is their dogma that Christianity is to blame for everything and

has never befriended the cause of humaneness. [131]

Environmental organisations explicitly or implicitly pledged to animal rights will, given half a chance, not hesitate for a second to destroy human livelihoods and cultures. The so-called seals war shows the morals of animal rights in action. No quarter given. Such really is the thrust hiding behind pussyfooting like:

Philosophical veganism espouses a reverence for the totality of life. [137]

Nuts

Vegetarianism is central to the understanding of animal rights. It is the most obvious practical consequence of their implementation. No vegetarianism, no animal rights. Full-blooded philosophical vegetarianism is a force in the anti-angling movement to be reckoned with, and for this reason we must look at vegetarianism and veganism. To begin with, it is useful to consider the definitions given by the International Vegetarian Union:

> *Vegetarian: For the purpose of membership of IVU, vegetarianism includes veganism and is defined as the practice of not eating meat, poultry or fish or their by-products, with or without the use of dairy products or eggs.*[115]

A "pescetarian"[116] is similar to a vegetarian but consumes fish – and he is, strictly speaking, not a vegetarian but a pseudo-vegetarian. Vegans go a step further inasmuch as they also prohibit the use or wearing of any animal products such as leather, silk or wool.

It's only since 1847 that vegetarianism has been called vegetarianism. Before it was known as the "Pythagorean System" after the Greek mathematician Pythagoras (c. 565 – c. 504 BC). "All is number", Pythagoras held, meaning that the universe can be grasped with mathematical formulae. Mathematics is one of the many sides of Pythagoras. Another one is his religious teaching, which involved specific advice such as:

> *… wise men ought not to sacrifice animals to the gods, nor yet to eat what has life, or beans, nor to drink wine.*[117]

Beans? Yes, beans. And here is why:

> *And it is said that Zaratas forbade men to eat beans because he said that at the beginning and composition of all things when the earth was still a*

---

115 http://www.ivu.org / This is a very good and informative site which doesn't just blast propaganda at you. It is biased, of course, but all the same it helps you understand what vegetarianism is all about.
116 Ibid.
117 Ibid.

*whole, the bean arose. And he says that the proof of this is that if one
chews a bean to pulp and exposes it to the sun for a certain time (for the
sun will affect it quickly) it gives out the odour of human seed. And he
says there is another clearer proof: if when a bean is in flower we were to
take the bean and its flower, and putting it into a pitcher moisten it and
then bury it in the earth, and after a few days dig it up again, we should
see in the first place that it had the form of a womb, and examining it
closely we should find the head of a child growing with it.* [118]

I am not the first nor the last to be baffled by this. Paul Strathern, in a
great little book about Pythagoras, presents an interesting angle:

*The ancient commentator Aulus Gellius offered an ingenious explanation
of Pythagoras' ban on eating beans. According to him what Pythagoras
had actually said was: 'Wretches, utter wretches keep your hands from
beans!' – which didn't mean quite what it seemed. In earlier times, beans
had been a euphemism for testicles, and thus Pythagoras' ban in fact
related to sexual activity. So either way, this would seem to be balls.* [119]

We don't know whether or not Elsie Shrigley and Donald Watson had an
interest in geometry and beans but we do know that they were the founders
of the Vegan Society in London in 1944.

Most vegetarians today except maybe a few diehards would agree with
John McArdle:

*Humans are classic examples of omnivores in all relevant anatomical traits.
There is no basis in anatomy or physiology for the assumption that
humans are pre-adapted to the vegetarian diet. For that reason, the best
arguments in support of a meat-free diet remain ecological, ethical and
health concerns.* [120]

This would seem to be a perfectly good thing. There is however a lot of
philosophy and politics in this diet. As in any movement, you'll find
moderates and hotheads. While the moderates seem to be perfectly happy to

118 Ibid.
119 Paul Strathern, *Pythagoras and his Theorem*, Arrow Books, London (1997), p.81. Pythagoras
was a most extraordinary man, "the first mathematician and philosopher in the Western world".
120 http://www.beyondveg.com John McArdle, an anatomist and primatologist, is a vegetarian and
scientific advisor to the American Anti-Vivisection Society.

let you continue fishing, the young Turks see the matter differently – like Singer and Regan do. Make no mistake about their intentions:

> ... prejudices die hard, all the more so when, as in the present case, they are insulated by widespread customs and religious beliefs, sustained by large and powerful economic interests, and protected by the common law. To overcome the collective entropy of these forces-against-change will not be easy. The animal rights movement is not for the faint of heart. Success requires nothing less than a revolution in our culture's thought and action. [121]

This is fairly explicit and the following is unequivocal:

> The ultimate objective of the rights view is the total dissolution of the animal industry as we know it. [122]

Certainly angling is not top of the agenda but it is not at the very bottom either – there is, after all, a sizeable angling industry with a vital interest in the fate of the sport. Is vegetarianism a threat to angling? In its animal rights form, most certainly yes. Somebody who opts for the vegetarian or vegan way based on motives generated by animal rights is bound to be an anti-angler. In order to exclude any misunderstanding about which type of vegetarianism, here's the list of those who are not necessarily anti-angling. Mind you, they are potential sympathisers of the animal rights cause.

1. Vegetarians for health reasons: These vegetarians simply believe that a vegetarian diet is healthier. They are not necessarily committed to animal rights.

2. Culinary objectors: These are the people who are not happy with the quality of meat products. They are temporary vegetarians and most likely the angler's friend.

3. Protest vegetarians: Those who have strong objections to the structures of the modern agri-business, (factory farming is the key term

---

121 Tom Regan, *The Case for Animal Rights*, University of California Press, Berkeley and Los Angeles CA (1985), Epilogue
122 http://www.furcommission.com

here); They are not necessarily committed to animal rights.

4. Compassionate vegetarians: These simply can't bear the thought of eating meat; they feel sorry for the creature but they are not necessarily committed to animal rights.

5. Religious vegetarians (ascetics): They are not necessarily committed to animal rights.

We now turn our attention to the hotheads who are fully committed to animal rights. That corner produces ideas like the "Animal rights Quote-o-Matic" on the Internet. The quote for January 2001 was:

Six million Jews died in concentration camps, but six billion broiler chickens will die this year in slaughter houses. Ingrid Newkirk, PETA[123]

This monstrosity is beyond belief. Yet it exists. The Holocaust, the attempt to exterminate a human culture, is attributed the same status as the slaughtering of broiler chickens in one year. In other words the death of a chicken equals a that of a human – there is no difference between them. Here you have Singerian "equal consideration" in its purest form, the true face of animal liberation.

The foundation for this sort of thing is laid by philosophers like Regan, Singer and others who spice their arguments with historical examples and comparisons of all sorts. History provides punchy instant insights. Another instance of this is the following passage from *Animal Liberation*:

It may seem that the period of the Renaissance, with the rise of humanist thought in opposition to medieval scholasticism, would have shattered the medieval picture of the universe and brought down with it earlier ideas about the status of humans vis-à-vis other animals.[124]

This is of great impressionistic simplicity. Brilliant sales talk. A few lines further Singer happily carries on:

So the Renaissance writers wrote self-indulgent essays in which they said that 'nothing in the world can be found that is more worthy of admiration

123 http://www.animalrights.net / Washington Post, (November 13, 1993), PETA.
124 Peter Singer, *Animal Liberation*, Avon Books, New York (1991), p.198.

than man' and described humans as 'the center of nature, the middle of the universe, the chain of the world'.[125]

To the not-so-informed about the Renaissance, this must make it look as though people at that time had nothing else to do but write self-indulgent essays all the time, forgetting all the while about animal rights. Renaissance scholars would no doubt be happy to learn that all there was to their subject was the writing of self-indulgent essays. Had Singer written, for example, "Some Renaissance writers wrote self-indulgent essays...", it would have been at least an attempt to do justice to the subject matter. Singer's flippancy might make great rhetoric but on closer inspection, as in the case of evolution and fairy tales, it has flaws. There is method in this kind of persuasive and elegant misrepresentation of historical facts and present-day realities – it's well-informed distortion: presenting as fact what is pure speculation or invention. It inevitably finds willing but less skilful imitators as we have seen above. And luckily for Renaissance culture and Europe, Singer wasn't around then telling everybody what to do.

Another example of instant eye-catching historical insight in the service of animal rights is slavery. Ever since *Animal Liberation*, slavery has been very popular with animal rights activists. No book, no pamphlet, no argument omits a sweeping comparison between farming or whatever and slavery. A masterpiece of historical and philosophical shoddiness is *The Dreaded Comparison* by Marjorie Spiegel. The final paragraph of the foreword by Alice Walker claims:

The animals of the world exist for their own reasons. They were not made for humans any more than black people were made for whites or women for men. This is the essence of Ms. Spiegel's cogent, humane and astute argument, and it is sound.[126]

Pretentious nonsense. Typically the book focuses on racial slavery in the United States. The reason for this is simple: the communicative power of certain cleverly selected facts makes convincing propaganda. The visual comparison of the treatment of slaves and the seemingly same treatment of animals today is indeed a great idea. The appeal goes straight to the heart.

125 Ibid., p.199.
126 Marjorie Spiegel, *The Dreaded Comparison*, Mirror Books, New York (1996).

Full marks. But what do we learn about slavery as such? What about the origins of slavery? Who exactly were the partners in crime? Is there, was there slavery elsewhere?

What about slavery in the Renaissance, for example, or in mediaeval Scandinavia? What about slavery, slaves and their treatment in non-Western societies? What about slavery today? What about non-racial slavery? There are no answers. *The Dreaded Comparison* is modelled on *Animal Liberation*. It contains some home truths, more half-truths and the full range of Singerian dogma. On top of that you'll be interested to learn that being a fisherman marks you as predisposed to slave-holding.[127]

The temptation to link slavery uniquely and exclusively to Christianity and Europe and to liken it to animals' fate today is so intense that even honest but somehow gullible traders, like Andrew Linzey[128], are attracted to it. Scratching the flashy surface of the interpretations of racial slavery might reveal that the facts don't suit the case. On top of that there might be too much serious intellectual effort and historical graft involved. The slaves/animals comparison as used by animal rightists glosses over the fact that slaves are human beings and animals are animals. The significance of this can't be emphasised enough. Of course, attempts have been made to "animalise" slaves but

Various Greek philosophers, especially the Cynics and the Stoics, saw a fundamental contradiction in trying to reduce any human being to such a subordinate status. "It would be absurd" Diogenes of Sinope reportedly said, when his own slave had run away, "if Manes [the slave] can live without Diogenes, but Diogenes cannot get on without Manes." When pirates captured Diogenes and took him to a slave market in Crete, he pointed to a customer wearing rich purple robes, and said: "Sell me to this man; he needs a master." Externally, according to the Stoics, the servant might be the instrument of his master's will, but internally, in his own self-consciousness, he remained a free soul.

---

127 Ibid., p.27.
The whole paragraph reads: "Yet even if some vast, undeniable distinction between humans and animals could finally be found, would that mean that we could then justify using, mistreating, even torturing, animals? Could we then say, as did eighteenth-century writer Thomas Love Peacock that 'nothing could be more obvious, than that all animals were created solely and exclusively for the use of man'? From any perspective other than one predisposed to slave-holding, we could not; that special, mythical quality or attribute that was the sole domain of humans would still be irrelevant."
128 Andrew Linzey, *Animal Gospel*, Westminster John Knox Press, Kentucky (2000), p.21.

In other words the master's identity depended on having a slave who recognised him as master, and this in turn required an independent consciousness. Contrary to Aristotle and in contrast to the relationship between a man and his dog, the roles of master and slave could be reversed: Diogenes could become the slave and Manes, who even as a slave might have had a freer soul and been less enslaved to his passions, could become the master.
This is the basic "problem of slavery" and it arises from the irreducible humanness of the slave.[129]

The indiscriminate slaves/animals comparison reduces slaves and slavery to cannon fodder for the cause of animal rights. This is particularily offensive and malicious because slavery far from being eradicated is still a major problem.[130] Hiding behind a facade of scientificness and compassion, *The Dreaded Comparison* like hundreds of other books in that vein turns out to be simply half-baked.

Historical mumbo-jumbo in the context of animal rights, vegetarianism and some environmentalism is rampant. This in itself wouldn't be of interest but the philosophical and political arguments are to a large extent based on historical "facts" and dubious interpretations of history. Another fine example of this is the assumption that Christian people have always been cruel oppressors of animals. Henry S. Salt leaves no doubt about this pernicious influence:

Religion has never befriended the cause of humaneness. Its monstrous doctrine of eternal punishment and the torture of the damned underlies much of the barbarity with which man has treated man; and the deep division imagined by the Church between the human being with his immortal soul, and the soulless "beasts", has been responsible for an incalculable sum of cruelty.[131]

One doesn't need to be a historian to ask questions. How then did animals fare before Christianity and what is their lot outside the Christian world, for example? Was it Christians who invented the maltreatment of animals? How widespread was cruelty two thousand years ago, really? This

---

129 Brian Davis, *In the Image of God*, Yale University Press (2001), pp.129–130.
130 See *Disposable People*, by Kevin Bales, University of California Press (2000).
131 http://ivu.org/history/salt/texts.html / Henry S. Salt is a remarkable figure and his *Animals' Rights* published in 1892 is an interesting book, to say the least.

question is of particular interest. Salt's remarks, like practically all other historical comments by animal rights writers, somehow seem to take it for granted that Christian man's treatment of animals can only be cruel. The people in charge of animals, we are told, have always woken up in the morning full of good Christian resolutions concerning the torture of the animals in their care. This is absurd, for many reasons, but the most obvious one is that most people aren't cruel.

Salt's wholesale collective guilt allocation and Singer's lament that man (mankind, Renaissance scholars) should know better show – in beautiful technicolour – what history means to animal rightists and militant vegetarians. It's a buffet and you help yourself to whatever suits your case. Intellectually it's uninformed, dishonest, distorted and arbitrary.

The cuddle

Vegetarianism is the *sine qua non* of a morally blameless life – no misunderstandings possible there. From Regan to Singer to PETA, no vegetarianism means no animal rights and no morally proper life. What then about societies like the Inuit? Are they to turn vegetarian? This is the moment of truth. The masks fall. The true face of animal rights and its vegetarian and vegan supporters is revealed.

Alan Herscovici explains what happened:

In October 1983, the European Economic Community banned the import of sealskin products. It was the climax of a long international protest campaign that made Greenpeace a household name and established doe-eyed "whitecoat" pups as the symbol of growing concern about protecting nature.

Rarely mentioned in the stacks of sensationalised reports that trace the twenty-year "seal wars", however, were the people who had most to lose in this debate – although they lived thousands of miles from the ice floes of Newfoundland and didn't even hunt harp-seal pups.

Seals (mainly ringed seals) had always provided food, clothing and other essentials for Inuit living in small camps along the vast arctic coasts. In the 1950s, however, government policies to improve health and educational facilities resulted in Canadian Inuit being resettled in larger communities, often far from traditional hunting grounds.

By good fortune new tanning methods developed in the 1960s allowed sealskins to be used for commercial fur garments, boosting international demand and prices. NWT ringed-seal skins, worth barely $1.00 before 1961, were bringing $14.00 per pelt in 1966. This money was used to buy supplies from the south, including power boats, gasoline, and snowmobiles that allowed Inuit hunters to travel farther and bring back more food for their communities.

A first wave of anti-sealing protests (sparked by the 1964 broadcast of a film about the Atlantic "whitecoat" hunt) reduced pelt prices to about

$4.00 by 1968, and U.S. markets were closed by the Marine Mammals Protection Act, in 1972. But European markets grew and prices rose steadily again through the 1970s, reaching record levels in 1976 ($24.00 per pelt). That year, seal-skin sales brought over one million dollars into the twenty-nine Inuit villages across the NWT. Even more valuable, the seal hunt produced 1.5 million kilos of meat – food that was more nutritious and far less expensive than imported supplies available from remote northern stores.

It appeared that fashion markets for sealskins would allow arctic Inuit to successfully adapt their culture and economy to their new conditions. By selling sealskins (a by-product of local food production), Inuit could enjoy modern health care, education and other advantages of living in larger communities, while maintaining their economic autonomy and hunting-based traditions. Service or industrial jobs remained scarce in remote northern communities, but no Inuit hunter was "unemployed" during this period.

Protests against the Atlantic "whitecoat" hunt reached new levels of intensity over the next few years, however, as Brigitte Bardot and Greenpeace arrived on the scene to bolster a campaign launched by Brian Davies' International Fund for Animal Welfare (IFAW).

At first, most Inuit ignored the publicity battles on Canada's east coast: Inuit hunted adult ringed seals, with harpoons or rifles; they didn't club harp-seal pups. The Inuit hunted for survival. They didn't feel "cut off from nature" and they needed no lessons in environmental awareness. This quarrel among competing groups of inscrutable white folks was a Qallunaat problem: Inuit assumed that it wouldn't affect them. They were wrong. Prices for NWT sealskins crashed in 1977. A brief resurgence in 1980/82 was snuffed out for good with the 1983 European import ban.

The impact on NWT communities which relied heavily on sealskin sales was swift and harsh: Broughton Islanders saw their total cash income drop from $92,000 to $13,500 in two years. In Pagnirtung, collective income fell from $200,000 to about $42,000 from 1981/82 to 1983/84. In the high Arctic community of Resolute, income slipped from $55,000 to $2,400. In all, the combined annual earnings of NWT Inuit hunters from sealskin sales are now estimated at perhaps $17,000 compared up to $1 million as recently as 1981.

*Income statistics, however, barely suggest the far-reaching nutritional, social, and cultural consequences of cutting hunters off from the land. Without money from sealskin sales to pay for equipment, gas and repairs, hunters can no longer provide sufficient meat for their communities. Increased consumption of store-bought processed and "junk" food brings serious health problems. Men who were autonomous hunters just ten years ago have been reduced to relying on welfare payments.
Those who do find wage employment have less time to hunt. Complex food-sharing relationships which reinforced social integration therefore break down as does the transmission of traditional skills and knowledge, the heart of culture.*

Hunters can no longer serve as role models or tutors for young people, many of whom now spend their days "hanging out" at the store without direction or hope. As Rhoda Inuksuk, then president of Inuit Tapirisat of Canada told the Parliamentary Standing Committee on Aboriginal Affairs,

One of the disasters that has happened as a result is youth suicide ... we have youth problems, drug and alcohol abuse, violence. There is very little employment and when you are hit with something like (the loss of sealskin markets) you are bound to see these problems come up as a result ...

According to Holman Island hunter David Omingmak, 'The life has been taken away from the people, and they don't know why.'

The world moves on. With media strategies and fund-raising techniques honed during the 'seals-wars' animal-rights campaigners have turned their sights on new targets: trappers, medical research, animal agriculture. In the words of Stephen Best, a former IFAW campaign organiser, a new 'protest industry' was born; it is now possible to pursue a career as a 'professional animal-rights activist.'

The world moves on. Brian Davies denies that it was hypocritical to destroy the livelihood of Inuit hunters, although he continues to eat meat and collects a six-figure salary and expenses. (The financial structure of IFAW's international affiliates is so complex that it is difficult to determine his full remuneration). Patrick Moore, president of Greenpeace at the peak of the 'seals wars', is now a commercial salmon farmer in British Columbia.

The world moves on. Brigitte Bardot recently alienated European environmentalists with her (fourth) marriage to an extreme right-wing French politician. Meanwhile, fish stocks are collapsing and some Atlantic seals receive contraceptive injections at tax-payers' expense, while health services for Canadian women are cut back.

Animal-rights activists claim to be ushering in a new era of moral concern to be "widening the circle of compassion". They call for a "new ethic" to control the relentless advance of science and technology that threatens human culture and nature. But for the Inuit, animal-rights campaigns are just the latest in a long litany of religious, industry and government policies imposed by outsiders – policies which ignore Inuit values and realities, and threaten the survival of one of the world's last remaining aboriginal hunting cultures.[132]

The following poem by Marie Van Katwyk and a song by Orpingalik, a Netsilik Eskimo man, show probably better than any reasoning how far worlds can be apart.

To a Baby Seal

Little baby white as snow,
Cuddled by your protecting mother,
Not knowing the fate befalling you,
There are cruel humans who want your fur,
To make fur coats for vain human-beings,
People who do not care
That your short life will end
In suffering and torture.
Men will come and club you to death,
And take your fur, then leave your
Skinned bleeding body for your mother
To mourn over.
But, little one there are some
Humans who care for you,
And other babies like you,
They fight to stop the cruelty,

---

132 http://www.furcouncil.com Alan Herscovici is the author of *Second Nature: the animal rights controversy*, CBC (1985), Stoddart, Toronto (1991). This is the first serious critique of the animal rights movement from a social and environmental perspective.

One day there will be an end,
To the suffering of all creatures,
Animals and Humans will live
In harmony with nature.
It will happen!
One day.[133]

This is pure compassion, it is sincere and genuine. However, also one of the caring people is the above-mentioned Stephen Best who is quoted as saying:

The Native people have got to become self-sufficient. They have got to have their own culture that is living. I own the Native culture. I bought it with my taxes. I own about two-thirds of it.[134]

Very appropriate also Tom Regan:

In issuing its condemnation of established cultural practices, the rights view is not antibusiness, not antifreedom of the individual, not antiscience, not antihuman. It is simply projustice, insisting only that the scope of justice be seen to include the rights of animals.[135]

And remember Singer's "logically cogent case that cannot be refuted."[132] which also means vegetarianism and the end of all animal-based or animal-related cultures or economies. Read the above poem again and let the message sink in and then read Orpingalik's song, also twice – and then draw your own conclusions:

My Breath

This is what I call my song, because it is as important for me to sing it, as it is to draw breath.

This is my song: a powerful song.
Unaija-unaija.

---

133 http://www.all-creatures.org/poetry/ar-babyseal.html
134 See *Animal Rights, Human Rights / Ecology, Economy and Ideology in the Canadian Arctic,* by George Wenzel, University of Toronto Press (2000), p.159.
135 Tom Regan, op.cit., Epilogue.

Since autumn I have lain here,
helpless and ill,
as if I were my own child.

Sorrowfully, I wish my woman
to another hut,
another man for refuge,
firm and safe as the winter-ice.
Unaija-unaija.

And I wish my woman
a more fortunate protector,
now I lack the strength
to raise myself from bed.
Unaija-unaija.

Do you know yourself?
How little of yourself you understand!
Stretched out feebly on my bench,
my only strength is my memories.
Unaija-unaija.

Game! Big game,
chasing ahead of me!
Allow me to re-live that!
Let me forget my frailty,
by calling up the past!
Unaija-unaija.

I bring to the mind that great white one,
the polar bear,
approaching with raised hind-quarters,
his nose in the snow –
convinced, as he rushed at me,
that of the two of us,
he was the only male!
Unaija-unaija.
Again and again he threw me down:
but spent at last,
he settled by a hump of ice,

and rested there,
ignorant that I was going to finish him.
He thought he was the only male around!
But I too was a man!
Unaija-unaija.

Nor will I forget that great blubbery one,
the fjord-seal, that I slaughtered
from an ice-floe before dawn,
while friends at home
were laid out like the dead,
feeble with hunger,
famished with bad luck.
I hurried home,
laden with meat and blubber,
as though I were just running across the ice
to view a breathing-hole.
Yet this had been an old and cunning bull,
who'd scented me at once –
but before he had drawn breath,
my spear was sinking
through his neck.

This is how it was.
Too sick to even fetch
a little seal oil for my woman's lamp.
Time, time scarcely seems to pass,
though dawn follows dawn,
And spring approaches the village
Unaija-unaija.

How much longer must I lie here?
How long? How long must she go begging
oil for the lamp,
reindeer-skins for her clothes,
And meat for her meal?
I, a feeble wretch:
She, a defenceless woman.
Unaija-unaija.

Do you know yourself?
How little of yourself you understand!
Dawn follows dawn,
and spring is approaching the village.
Unaija-unaija.[136]

The victims are identifiable, some of the profiteers too. Then something extraordinary and important happens: it becomes blurred who is responsible for what. Activists at the front excuse themselves by their conscience and their mandate from whatever organisation. The managers hide behind the mandate of their organisations and will disclaim any personal responsibility. In turn the governing bodies of the organisations in question will point to their charters and the mandate given to them by their donors. The donors, if challenged, will then say that they thought they supported the good cause for which the organisation stands – everybody is passing on the hot potato and in the end, predictably, it will be the victim's own fault.

When focusing on the Inuit in the story of the seal war, one must not forget that there is also the side of the Newfoundland sealers who were at the centre of the storm. Their voice has completely gone under and so have the original reasons for the seal cull. I have chosen the Inuit perspective because they weren't in the picture at all at the beginning. They were simply ignored and then victims in a war of compassion. No troops required – a seal fur ban is more efficient. The Inuit don't even have the chance to fight. This is not the place to discuss the issue in detail. It's like in angling: if fishing is fundamentally wrong, then all of it is wrong, regardless of the tactics. Clubbing, shooting, whatever are merely side issues. The questions are more basic: is it right to use animals? Is wildlife management right?

In their "…condemnation of established cultural practices", animal rights activists give enormous scope to their movement. They certainly won't run out of causes. Think of cultures and economies which depend on animals: Iceland, the Faroe Islands and all the nomadic pastoralists in Africa and Central Asia. What are those people supposed to do? Just disappear like that? Yes. And it's no accident. It's the logic of veganism which clearly states that:

136 Tom Lowenstein, *Eskimo Poems from Canada and Greenland*, Pittsburgh University Press, (1973), pp. 38–40.

mollusks and all sea animals are diverse and unique creatures whose right to live freely, unencumbered by human interference, is acknowledged and respected by the vegan ethic. There is every scientific reason to believe these animals value their lives, as do all sentient beings, feel pain, demonstrate fear, and want to live. Philosophic veganism espouses a reverence for the totality of life. This conviction includes sea animals no less than any others.[137]

If this philosophy is translated into universal reality (and that is what it aims at) there is no room for compromise as far as human beings are concerned. The only permitted attitude to animals will be compassion.

The Faroe Islands, huddled in the stormy North Atlantic midway between Norway and Iceland, regularly make the headlines for two reasons. The first one is their national football team. Like their Viking forebears this amateur team strikes terror among the European multi-million-euro national sides. Regularly they bring reputed European football nations not just to the brink of disaster – their victories have made football history. The second headline-making reason is the whale hunt: the hunt for pilot whales (not an endangered species). This is a traditional hunt, embedded in the culture of the Faroe Islands and a welcome supplement on the table. Fish and sheep are the pillars of the economy – the moral worst-case scenario from the animal rights point of view. The people of the Faroe Islands will either have to eat grass or emigrate if the animal rights movement has its way. Animal rightists are working on it.

The nice people from the International Fund for Animal Welfare, of Inuit fame, probably looking for new causes with fund-raising potential, first lashed out at the Faroe Islands back in 1985. Greenpeace US also thought there might be something in it but they and the IFAW withdrew after a while. Since then an organisation called "Sea Shepherd International" and some smaller organisations are trying hard, unfairly and dangerously, to bring the Faroe Islands into disrepute. The important action takes place in boardrooms and parliamentary lobbies in England, Germany and other European countries. It's all so beautifully anonymous.

The script looks familiar: encouraged by politicians and animal rights movements the brainless politically correct are duly scandalised by the

---

137 Joanne Stepaniak, *Being Vegan*, Lowell House, Los Angeles, (2000), p.31.

Faroese whaling and will agree to boycott Faroes products. It's simple; you don't even have to do anything! It's the seal fur story in another guise. None of the politicians, teachers, parents and kids will have had a direct hand in actively depriving the Faroese of their culture or in making their lives harder than it already is. It's all clean. Everyone can wash their hands in innocence, should it one day become clear that, in fact, one has participated in the business of sinking people into poverty in the name of animal rights.

The moral charges against the traditional Faroese pilot whale hunt have a familiar ring to them. The accusers call it cruel, outdated, unnecessary and claim:

There is no place for this in the modern world.[138]

They might as well say "There is no place for the Faroese people in the modern world." That is essentially what it boils down to. In the case of the Faroe Islands there is also a kind of inverted racism coming into play. While many people would concede the right to hunt to the Inuit they would deny it to the Faroese, for they are blond-haired, blue-eyed and European. The fact that the Faroese are a modern nordic people is stressed time and again in the anti-whaling propaganda.

The little defence there is of a philosophy which allows for depriving people of their livelihood and culture under the banner of animal rights runs along the following lines:

I am sympathetic to special considerations of some local autonomy, self-policing, local administration, etc. being given to indigenous peoples. However, I also believe that some values are too important to make them merely optional or local. There are some universal principles of justice or preferred ways of living that we ought to defend and promote.[139]

The people of the Faroe Islands are clearly an obstacle to a universal principle concerning animals. That's pure Regan – a bit less sophisticated but there's that same condescending concern and the *ex cathedra* pronouncement of "universal principles". The outcome is the same: any resistance in the philosophical or the real world will be steamrollered.

138 http://www.cnn.com/2000/NATURE/09/11/faroe.islands.enn/
139 http://articles.animalconcerns.org/ar-voices/archive/native.html#low. This does not directly refer to the Faroese case but is presented as general justification to persecute native cultures. A document of outrageous conceit.

It doesn't need to be an entire culture in order to serve as a target. A town will do: Bucharest. Literally hundreds of thousands of stray dogs plague the town (the estimates vary between 100,000 and 300,000).[140] A 62-year-old man was savaged to death by dogs and every day thousands of people are bitten. When the mayor decided to do something about the situation, a howl of indignation went around animal rights organisations all through Europe. To prevent the cull, Brigitte Bardot stirred the emotions, other organisations sent equipment and personnel for sterilisations, petitions were sent, other people still wanted to adopt dogs (requests came from as far as Los Angeles). The apparatus of compassion was in full swing. The arguments were the all-familiar animal rights lore: again philosophy in action. And again, once the dust has settled, what remains? The street kids and orphans will still be there, poverty will still be a major problem, and people will still starve. In the meantime Brigitte Bardot, with the rejuvenated conscience of a hundred thousand saved dogs, looks for the next cause in this vanity fair of compassion.

Philosophical vegetarianism and veganism entail the abolition of angling. In a different league and one hundred percent pro-angling are the culinary objectors. They object to poor quality products. It's like those people who prefer to drink no wine at all rather than to drink bad wine. Life is too short for bad wine. Vegetarianism of the pragmatic or discerning kind is not anti-angling. Uneasiness or disapproval of factory farming is not anti-angling.

Whether they like it or not, vegetarians and anglers are allies. They must have a concern for the methods of food production. Take, for example, fertilisers: their type and use are of the highest interest to the angler and the vegetarian alike. On a lake around which there is farming, the "wrong" fertiliser (being washed in by rain) can have a negative impact on fishing, soil and the product being grown on it. The point is: anglers and vegetarians, ethical or pragmatic, share a common concern about the environment. Strange bedfellows they make, but there you are.

140 Kate Conolly, The Guardian (28 February 2001).
    BBC News (2 March 2001).
    Reuters (4 November 2001).
    See also: http://www.dogsinthenews.com/issues/0103/articles/010320c.htm

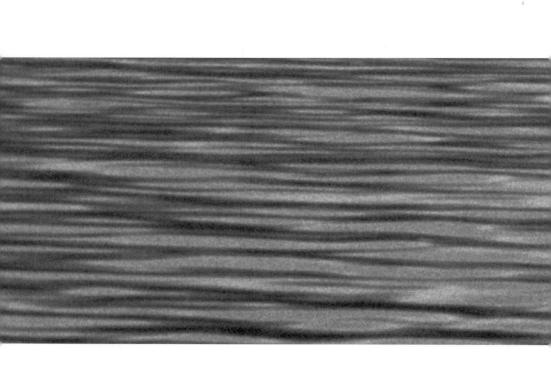

Chapter 6

SHORT CUT

These days everybody is an environmentalist. You'll have a hard time finding somebody who would bluntly tell you that he is not all for it. For what, exactly? It's such a multi-faceted idea that it is hard to grasp what it is all about in the first place. It's certainly a flexible concept. Common to most modern radical environmentalism is an underlying assumption that man is basically undesirable, an idea shared with animal rights philosophies. That's extraordinary because the very people telling you this usually believe in evolution which should tell them that man is part of nature. He can on no account not belong there. And he certainly can't be blamed for being a successful species.

Environmentalism comes in all shapes and guises. It's the sort of idea which lends itself to individual moulding. Anybody can make up his own philosophy and feel good about it. Conservation is a puzzling idea. The very word suggests that there is something to conserve, yet the nature of nature is that it constantly changes. If you look at a mountain, all seems solid rock. Yet as the seconds tick away it is being eroded. Yesterday's rocky mountains are today's sandy beaches. You can't conserve a mountain.

Save the planet, kill yourself![156]

At this radical end of the spectrum there is no room for angling. The people here tend to be in accord with full-blooded animal rights. I hesitate to say so for fear of being boring, but I've got to: in the eyes of radical environmentalists it is, again, Christianity at the root of all evil.

Alliances between environmental and animal rights groups are not uncommon. Often, in fact, an animal rights campaign appears in the guise of a conservation issue. The story of the cormorant is a fine example. Mainstream environmentalism is not necessarily anti-angling. One reason coming into play is that anglers are potential donors to environmental organisations.

Nature isn't what it used to be – it never was. Yet quite a few scientists and philosophers think they have understood it all and know the right course to steer:

A thing is right when it preserves the integrity, stability and beauty of the biotic community.[144]

"Biotic community" means the community of living things. On such a basis, anything in politics and society goes. This line of thinking used to be called fascism. Today it's called ecocentrism. Fishing is okay as long as it isn't seen by the biotic dictatorship to have a negative influence on the biotic community.

One

Conserving natural resources, preventing pollution and controlling land use are the hallmarks of environmentalism, which comes in all shapes and sizes. Environmentalists are not necessarily anti-angling. The alternative environmental movement deserves credit for having drawn the attention of a wider public to the urgency of various problems. Part of this success was due to the inertia of the traditional organisations concerned in the widest sense with nature and animal welfare. These organisations failed to generate enthusiasm among young people. Greenpeace and others spoke the language of youth. Since the 1970s the movement has gained enormous momentum and grown to a conglomerate of thousands of national and international organisations.

Everybody nowadays is to some degree environmentally aware. This sensibility has, for example, translated into various anti-pollution laws and the treatment of waste. A perfectly good thing on the whole, and it's bound to continue because politicians have seen the voter potential – and the businessmen the opportunities. What I describe here is a sort of rational, more or less scientifically based, mainstream environmental concern. Specific problems like sewage, pig slurry, fertiliser and so on are looked into and solved according to the best present-day know-how. It's an ongoing concern and a good thing too, because it tends to benefit all those involved. In town and country alike. This is not to say that all is bliss, there are frictions and clashes between various interests. There is petty squabbling on ideological grounds. All this, however, is not of an irreconcilable nature. Most locally identifiable environmental problems can be solved because there is that basic consensus that it is desirable to solve such problems.

The moment environmentalism takes on national, continental or global dimensions, tone and attitude change. On that scale, confrontation seems to be inevitable – confrontation mostly between economic and environmental interests, as if they were mutually exclusive. Part of the reason is certainly that industry and politics in Europe and the United States understood far too late that there is a problem with, for example, carelessly dumping toxic waste. The mistrust of the promises given by big industries originates in the sins of the 50s, 60s and 70s.[141] The other source of strife lies in the competitiveness of the environmental business. What's the problem?

Environmental organisations[141] like those concerned with humanitarian causes have, apart from their mission, a business side. In Great Britain, for example, around a hundred big environmental charities compete with literally hundreds of thousands of other recognised charities for funds.[142]

The bigger an organisation, like Greenpeace, the stronger the financial pressures. Money is needed, lots of it, not just for projects but also for professional management. Part of successful charity marketing is public relations. Seals were great public relations. Equally good news is chained activists but, alas, the novelty of it is beginning to wear off. To make the news, the stunts become riskier and riskier and before long there will be serious injury or death. Another problem for environmental organisations is to keep the fire burning. The interest in old causes must be kept alive and new causes have to be found. No causes, no news – no funds. Confrontation obtains more exposure! There's something inexorable about the progress of these big organisations:

> ... Greenpeace has assumed some of the trappings of the global
> corporations it attacks. Recently it hired an Italian hilltop village and flew
> in the heads of its national operations for a week-long meeting on policies
> and campaign.[143]

Organisations such as Greenpeace need professional management and administration and the people there quite understandably have an interest in keeping their jobs. The issues that are consequently taken up by big environmental organisations aren't necessarily those with the greatest urgency (cf. the former Soviet bloc) but those which promise the most publicity.

The origins of today's environmentalism go back to the 19th century. In the United States writers like Emerson, Thoreau and Marsh and leaders like Gifford Pinchot prepared the ground for what is probably the most famous statement of environmentalism: 'The Land Ethic' by Aldo Leopold. 'The Land Ethic' is a powder-keg essay.

---

141 A really informative website which gives you a rundown of the environmental movement in the United States is http://www.ecotopia.org/ehof/timeline.html The links allow you to go as deep as you want. A treasure site!
142 See http://www.nao.gov.uk/pn/01-02/0102234.htm In 2002 there were 185,000 charities in the UK.
143 See http://www.greenpiece.org/index.html This website is very critical of Greenpeace. The source of the quote is given as the Sunday Times (30 July 2000).

Its very title is a challenge in the sense that one is immediately forced to ask oneself how land can have an ethic. It can't. The basic idea is that land and all its life, the "biotic community", should determine human ethics in the sense of it being the ultimate standard for judging whether or not actions are right or wrong. The key sentence in *The Land Ethic* is:

A thing is right when it tends to preserve the integrity, stability and beauty of the biotic community.[144]

The biotic community as the gold standard of these environmental ethics entails a lot of problems for human beings. That is if you like to see yourself as a person and not a biotic unit. The principal difficulty is that such ethics are flux ethics: stability here can only mean sufficient stability to change or adapt. A system without a minimum of stability is dead; this is what Leopold must mean, otherwise evolution wouldn't make sense in his world. Permanent change must be the rule because the requirements of the biotic community frequently change. That's the evolutionary lesson. It is very hard for the ordinary biotic citizen to know what at a given time is right or wrong. He needs to be told. The biological authorities will at any given time issue the moral policies in force. This deprives the individual not only of their freedom and responsibility but also of being considered a person in the conventional sense. Thus, the individual is more a biological unit. Should such a biological unit or group of such units pose a perceived threat to the "biotic community", they could and should, by land ethic standards, be disposed of. This used to be called fascism, today it's called ecocentrism or "deep ecology". The implications are the same. Leopold writes:

Conservation is a state of harmony between men and land.[145]

Included in this harmony are, implicitly, animal rights[146]. If the state of dynamic harmony (stability) is in presumed danger from human beings then human beings, will have to conform with whatever will bring back or supposedly promote that harmony. Theoretically this entails the possibility of animals enjoying more legal rights than human beings except, of course, the lawmakers. An unfriendly reading of 'The Land Ethic' has it simply that all would be hunky-dory in nature if it weren't for man. Especially recreational man who dares to leave the cities for rambling, biking, fishing,

144 Aldo Leopold, *A Sand County Almanac*, Ballantine Books, New York (1970), p.262.
145 Ibid., p.243.
146 Ibid., p.239.

hunting, bird watching – whatever he does out there is bound to be wrong. What the people who enjoy outdoor pursuits (not all do!) are supposed to do except stay indoors isn't quite clear in what Leopold says. There is, however, no uncertainty that outdoor pursuits tend to abuse land. The attitude allowing such allegedly misguided understanding of what nature is or should be about is, yet again, of biblical origin:

> *Conservation is getting nowhere because it is incompatible with our Abrahamic concept of land.*[147]

The reason why Christianity comes under permanent shelling is that it dares to be unashamedly anthropocentric in its teachings and ethics. Anthropocentric means to see the world primarily from the human point of view. The opposite pole is ecocentrism which focuses on all the things not human – i.e. animals, plants, environment, in a word – the ecosphere.[148] The human-centred Christian view is a world with a God. Ecocentric views tend to be godless and materialistic as in biological determinism. There is no room in nature for God – at least not for a Christian God.

The relentless caricaturing of Christianity as the bogeyman for all sorts of wrongs in history, philosophy and society is boring and destructive. Even if you're highly critical of Christianity or an arch-atheist, you can't just simply bin tradition, neither conceptually nor in reality. You can't jump over your own shadow. Dump Christianity and you dump not only culture but humanity with it. Christianity is religion and a great cultural achievement from which all of its critics draw the very energy they require to think up alternative models. Typically Regan and Singer want to stay in that general framework as far as its amenities go.

It's not altogether an idle thought to depict the constructs of philosophers like Regan and Singer as real buildings. Regan's philosophy to me clearly evokes the image of a millet silo decorated with water colours of flower-festooned guillotines. Singer's building you don't see really. His philosophy has the charm of a disused underground military hospital with blood-splattered walls. Now compare these buildings with a Gothic cathedral and draw your own conclusions. That is one side of it. The other is that if you

---

147 Ibid. xviii and p.240.
148 An excellent introduction is "Ecospheric Ethics", http://www.ecospherics.net / This site also shows how difficult it is to keep up with terminology.

don't find room for God in your philosophy in general, you miss a quintessential point about human beings. But who is interested in human beings...?

Back to Aldo Leopold. If you read him in an unfriendly way there are indeed many reasons to say that his views invite fascism. In a friendly reading in which one assumes that Leopold didn't see some of the implications of his arguments, you discover first a great nature writer. Aldo Leopold might not have been the most self-critical of ethical writers but he certainly knew his subject matter: nature. And he was a hunter and angler – there is a lovely fishing story in the Sand County Almanac which alone is worth the price of the book. Leopold is not an anti-angler; his mission is conservation and as such in principle he is the angler's friend. However, should angling in any way conflict with conservation, which in the eyes of contemporary radicals it invariably does, angling has to stop.

An intriguing variant of environmentalism is Gaia theory. Gaia is the name of the Greek Earth goddess. Gaia has received a lot of attention in the last thirty years or so. This is the gist of it:

For more than a century students of the evolution of the living and non living parts of the earth have known that life influences the physical and chemical characteristic of the planet. Nevertheless, the dominant paradigm in earth sciences has been that inexorable inorganic forces, such as changing energy output from the Sun, collisions of the Earth with extraterrestrial bodies, continental drift, or other orbital element variations have been the principal driving forces behind climate twenty years ago. James Lovelock and Lynn Margulis coined the phrase the Gaia hypothesis to suggest not only that life has a greater influence on the evolution of the Earth than is typically assumed across most earth science disciplines but also that life serves as an active control system. In fact they suggest that life on earth provides a cybernetic, homeostatic feedback system, leading to stabilisation of global temperature, chemical composition and so forth.

When first introduced in the early 1970s the Gaia hypothesis attracted the most attention from theologians interested in the possibility that the Earth controlled its environment on purpose (i.e., teleological implications), from those looking for 'oneness' in nature, and from those defending polluting industries, for whom the Gaia hypothesis provided a convenient excuse whereby some collective set of natural processes would largely offset any potential damages from human disturbance to earth systems. Although none of these aspects was underlined in the scientific work of Lovelock and Margulis, these nonscientific side issues diverted attention in the scientific community away from a serious analysis of the Gaia hypothesis and its implications. By the mid 1980s, Gaia advocates and detractors began a series of critiques and countercritiques, often carried out through third parties such as television documentary producers. One of us (Schneider) having been party to such a debate came to realise the absurdity of the situation in which an interesting and controversial idea like the Gaia hypothesis was being debated largely in nonscientific forums, if at all.[149]

There is a poetical side to Gaia too:

Gaia's elemental chant

Great mother Gaia become 1 with me ...

Become 1 with me
With Your earth as my body
1 with me
With my body as Your earth

1 with me
With Your air as my breath
1 with me
With my breath as Your air

1 with me
With Your fire as my passion
1 with me
With my passion as Your fire

1 with me
With your water as my blood
1 with me

---

149 http://ess.geology.ufl.edu/ess/Introduction/GAIA_hypothesis.html / and *Scientists on Gaia*, edited by Stephen Schneider and Penelope Boston, The MIT Press, Cambridge, MA (1991).

With my blood as Your water

1 with me
With Your spirit as my guide
1 with me
With my spirit as Your guide

Oh great Mother Gaia become 1 with me, 1 with me
1 with me

become 1 with me …

1 with me thru Your elemental energy

written thru & by savannah skye …[150]

I quite like this. It explains very lucidly what the Gaia theory is all about and by what "spirit" people who believe in it are driven. The tree huggers' chant in "my" forest could have been something like this poem which really is a pagan prayer. The original presentation somehow takes the sting out of its deadly seriousness. There's a lighthearted touch to this.

A very solemn spin-off of the Gaia theory is "deep ecology", a philosophy (ecosophy) which one finds through deep experience. The deep experience which is said to inspire ecosophs:

is the sense of intrinsic value in the unfolding of life's potential[151]

Intrinsic, inherent, innate, natural – one is never far away from these key words in discussions about animal rights or environmentalism. In the context of animal rights and deep ecology it invariably leads to conclusions, views and arguments which tend to focus on

pernicious anthropocentrism,[152]

---

150 http://www.craftswomen.com/wwwboard/messages/106.html
151 http://www.gn.apc.org/resurgence/185/harding185.htm
152 Ibid.

137

Christianity bashing and the wholesale condemnation of Western values. It is said, for example, that

we churn out scientists without philosophy, who are merely interested in their subject, but not thoroughly awed by it.[153]

There is a solution:

Gaian perception helps to remedy this great mental and spiritual plague, a malaise which has arisen in the West and which is now claiming millions of victims, human and non-human, throughout the world.[154]

Whatever is meant by that, it is by no means the limit. Here's the description of a bumper sticker of the Earth-First-Journal.

Slogan: More wilderness, less people.
Visual: Picture of a newborn baby with a slash through it.
Advertised as: Send a message to the breeders.[155]

The jewel in the crown in this line surely is the protester with the banner:

Save the planet, kill yourself![156]

No need to ask then whether or not angling is on.

At the moment the big environmental organisations tolerate anglers. After all they are potential donors whom one doesn't want to alienate unnecessarily. The situation for angling would obviously look radically different if animal rightists and fundamentalist environmentalists had their way. We said that the campaign for the abolition of angling is not about fish but about fishermen. A few million anglers and millions and millions of non-anglers (non-vegetarians) are, obviously, in the way of a harmonious all-problems-solved world which is just round the corner and the faster they're out of the way the better. The heart of the anti-angling matter is an all-encompassing change of values.

153 http://schumachercollege.gn.apc.org/articles/stephan.htm
154 Ibid.
155 http://www.off-road.com/green/chapter91.html
156 http://www.off-road.com/media/lycos_orig.html

Nature isn't what it used to be

The words 'conservation' and 'sustainable development' are like braces. They will hold up any pair of trousers. The most narrow sense to which one can pin down these words might be in terms of economics: the world's natural resources are limited and should be preserved or used in such a way that they will be available to future generations. On the face of it conservation seems a fairly straightforward, practical matter: one can weigh, count, calculate and so on. Conservation concerns angling in many ways. In the wider sense, conservation and sustainable development also are the pertinent parameters, for example, for the discussion of driftnets and ocean-floor hoovering. Another problem in which every angler everywhere will take an interest is pollution because regardless of where it happens, sooner or later it will have an effect in your neck of the woods.

All that seems crystal clear, but is it really? Conservation aims for a status quo to be preserved. Vast areas are chosen and declared as nature parks. Ordinary mortals are partly or totally banned from these sanctuaries, and there is usually a lot of talk about wilderness and preserving some important wildlife. A few chosen scientists have access to the zone in question – like high priests having sole access to the holy of holies. Here is an example of a description representative of many such sanctuaries:

> *Indiana's Nature Preserves are the real hidden treasures of the state. They have everything state parks have, and more – except people. With a few exceptions, the Nature Preserves are rarely visited; even when there are actually other people out there, you may never see them. If wildflowers or birds are in your line, this is the place to find the most unusual and interesting. The scenery can also be spectacular (for Indiana) and of interest. The Nature Preserve system is a collaboration between a number of groups and state agencies: the Nature Conservancy, ACRES; NICHES and other local and regional groups, universities, counties and the Department of Natural Resources have worked together to save the most unique and interesting pieces of Indiana. Many Nature Preserves are so fragile and protect such endangered species that visitation is restricted.*[157]

---

157 http://dcwi.com/~eric/goot/natpsrv.htm

This is a fine illustration of how deeply the idea has already taken root, that man is somewhat misplaced and even undesirable in nature. Don't get me wrong: Indiana's Nature Preserves are perfectly okay and I do support conservation projects because many of them make sense. What I am worried about is the underlying assumption that man is, by virtue of being man – worse still Western man – not a good idea in nature or nature reserves. If you wanted, you could modify the above text to make it sound more positive, extolling the virtues of a 'state of grace' landscape unpolluted by the presence of man. It would be much nicer, wouldn't it?

Think for a minute about landscape in this context. Most continental European landscape, for example, is man-made, especially that close to civilisation centres (civitas is the Latin word for town). The history of European forests dramatically illustrates this. The gist of it is that forests were exploited practically down to the last tree. Civilisation over the centuries was built on wood. Amsterdam and Venice and many other European cities are built on wooden poles. And think of paper, charcoal, mines, salt works, ship building; think of the smith, the baker and the cook – wood was the number-one raw material and energy source.

By the beginning of the 19th century it was realised that if nothing were done there would be no more forests left. Reforestation started and to put it sweepingly, today's nature conservation areas were planted 200 years ago. On top of that forests themselves had changed in the course of evolution, with some types of forest disappearing and others emerging. In short, forests and landscapes change with or without human influence and what you decide to conserve is always a snapshot, so to speak.

The opposite of park-type conservation is intervention – like the reforestation just mentioned. Man does at a given moment whatever at that time seems to be the right thing to do. In the case of European forests it looks as if planting trees was the wise decision. As in the case of forests there also has been a lot of "planting" of freshwater fish. Andrew Herd writes of the period in the second half of the 19th century:

> For twenty years it seemed that the oceans were criss-crossed with the wakes of ships playing an epic game of backgammon with our trout populations and so few records were kept that it is hard to keep track of what went where, save to say that the genetic pool became irretrievably mixed up. Sea trout eggs were exported to Australia as early as 1866;

*brook charr were sent to England in 1869 and New Zealand in 1877;
rainbows arrived in New Zealand in 1881 and in England in 1884; but
perhaps the most significant planting occurred in 1883, when a German
steamship called the Werra docked at the New York waterfront. It was an
unremarkable landing apart from one item on the ship's manifest: eighty
thousand brown trout eggs lying on cool moss lined trays.*[158]

The reason for this intervention was a sort of "reforesting" scheme.
The man who took the initiative, Fred Mather, was invited to fish in
Germany, where

*...it dawned on him that the shy brown trout he found there were ideally
situated to withstand the growing fishing pressure in the environs of cities
like New York and Philadelphia. The other attribute of the brown trout
that endeared them to Mather was their ability to cope with water
temperatures above seventy-five degrees, which convinced him that they
might do well in the rivers of the eastern watersheds, where the water
was slowly warming as a result of the devastating clear-felling that had
followed the American Civil War. The problem Mather was trying to
resolve was the impending loss of the cold-water-loving brook trout which
had been the cornerstone of American fly fishing until then.*[159]

The trout are but the tip of the iceberg. Over the centuries animals, trees
and all sorts of plants have travelled extensively. Sometimes with man's help
(intentional or unintentional); sometimes without it. The effect of all this to-
ing and fro-ing is that you'll find exotic introductions everywhere around the
globe – and you can't really be too certain what is what. How many
generations does it take to make a local out of an intruder? The point is that
on closer scrutiny nature and conservation, or nature and preservation, look
like a contradiction in terms. Unless, of course, you want to preserve nature
at a certain moment in time for it to follow its nature, which seems to be
change. But what happens if there is a biological invasion taking place – do
you intervene or do you leave nature to deal with the situation?

According to Tom Regan's animal rights doctrine there is no legitimate
way to interfere.[160] This strict non-interference principle would, for example,
mean that the sea lampreys of the Great Lakes should be left to wipe out the

---

158 Andrew Herd, *The Fly*, The Medlar Press Ltd, Ellesmere, England (2001), p.302.
159 Ibid., p.303.
160 Tom Regan, *The Case for Animal Rights*, University of California Press, Berkeley and Los
Angeles CA (1985), p.357.

whole lake-trout population there.[161] Conservation is a kind of intervention – after all, the heart of any conservationist scheme is to steer the course of events in a particular direction. Conservation sets the points. All this sounds, if a bit confusing, wonderfully acceptable and uncontroversial to the point of trivial until you start to think about what happened in the big cormorant issue. This is animal rights and environmentalism in action and it's the same telling story all over the fishing world.

For those happily not familiar with the story, here is an outline of the events: back in the Seventies the numbers of cormorants in Europe and the United States declined to such an extent that it was deemed necessary to put cormorants under protection. The birds took their chance admirably well and multiplied into huge colonies. So successful the cormorant proved that now fishermen see red when the black bird is mentioned.

Why?

The first indisputable fact of the story that sticks out like a sore thumb is the fishing fraternity's utter failure to stem the rising tide. There are three reasons for this – again it's the same story everywhere. One: the animal rights and conservation lobby was more effective. Small but influential. Two: the angling organisation officials up to about that time were at a bit of a loss as to how to deal with the new kind of activism. Some of them and many anglers (including myself) didn't see the implications. Officials and anglers at that time were mostly busy with questions concerning water pollution and protection of natural fish habitats. Ironically, the successful habitat work provided the feeding grounds for cormorants. The vital point is that anglers have never said that they wanted the cormorant extinct – all they ask is to keep things in reasonable proportion. Anglers have always been part of conservation projects. Anglers were conservationist before the word was invented, yet in all the documents I read relating to the cormorant issue, it's always conservation vs. anglers or cormorant vs. anglers or bird protection vs. anglers and so on.

Somehow angling itself or the anti-angling animal rights propaganda has managed to position the angler as a pure consumer, as a competitor for resources on a par with cormorants. This leads to the third reason: anglers

---

161 The source for information on the Great Lakes is: http://www.great-lakes.net
Lake Victoria and the introduction of the Nile perch there is another instance of a biological invasion. The story is very well told at: http://www.oneworld.org/patp/pap_victoria.html

are no longer creative participants in the general movement for the protection of nature. At least not in the public eye. A lot of valuable work is done in clubs and associations but the bitter fact must be faced: it's not good enough, not clever enough. Classrooms, lobbying halls and centre stage itself are taken by the animal rights and conservationist exponents.

The communications management by the anti-anglers and conservationists in the cormorant question is simply brilliant. For years they have been able to convince the public at large that there is no problem with the cormorant. A perfect ruse used practically everywhere are studies to establish facts which are staring everybody in the face. In this way, time has been gained and the cormorants have happily bred like rabbits. What are the facts of all the studies? The one undisputed reality is that the number of cormorants has increased beyond belief. In the Great Lake region of Canada and the US the number of cormorant nests grew from 89 to 38,000 between 1970 – 1991.[162] The numbers are equally staggering for Great Britain and continental Europe. In the lakes of Bavaria, for example, the cormorant was never heard of before 1980. Evidence of the depletion of fish stocks and the virtual extinction of fish life for miles, especially in rivers suited for the cormorants' type of hunt, is abundant. Yet time and again it is (still) said that all is hunky-dory. A fine example of skilful communication is a letter dated 14 June 2000 from Gerald W. Winegrad representing the American Bird Conservancy and other organisations to the US Fish and Wildlife Service. The subject of the letter is the following:

These comments are submitted on behalf of the American Bird Conservancy regarding the Notice of Intents to prepare an EIS[163] and National Management Plan for the Double-crested Cormorant ...

ABC and its associated organisations...

... pride themselves on applying science to bird conservation issues.

The letter goes on to say what might have been expected:

... there is no new biologically sound basis for concluding that a widespread population control effort for cormorants under a new

162 http://www.fishinghotpage.com/cormo4.htm
163 Environmental Impact Statement.

*management plan would be beneficial to aquaculture or any other
fish stocks.*

ABC touches only indirectly on the total number of cormorants
involved: 924,000, each of which gulps a pound of fish a day. Ten percent of
the cormorants may be legally taken out of circulation which still leaves a lot
of mouths (or rather, beaks) to be fed. The writer then takes us through the
whole spiel to conclude:

*Fish eating birds have co-existed with their prey species for many
thousands of years while both birds and fish flourished. The key difference
now is that human activities have greatly impaired the ability of fish to
survive.* [164]

That's a clever package: there is the appeal to science. The tone is matter-
of-fact, almost detached, underlining the scientificness of the cause and what
is being said. If however you scratch the surface a bit it becomes clear that the
letter is nothing more than a well-disguised programmatic statement telling
the Wildlife Service what it has to do. Apart from the typical self-
righteousness there is also the reiteration of an old theme: it's those blasted
humans again standing in the way of nature. In this case the fishermen
subgroup is at least partly responsible for the diminishing fish stocks and

164 http://www.abcbirds.org/policy/cormorant_letter.htm
The sources for these paragraphs on the cormorant question are : www.environment-agency.gov.uk /
http://pisces.enviroweb.org/corm.html / http://www.frep.com (January 10, 2002) /http://harbor-
watch.com (May/June 1997) / http://www.petri-heil.ch/diskurs//02-97.html /
http://www.fishingnj.org/artcormorant3.htm /
http://www.cormorantbusters.co.uk / http://www.fischnetz.ch /
http://fishinghotpage.com/cormo4.htm /
http://www.anti-angling.com/corm3.html / http://www.all-creatures.org/cash/cc99sp-
cormorants.html / and
http://www.audubon.org/news/release00/cormorants.html
M. Klein, "Neubewertung des Einflusses von Kormoranen auf Fischbestände in grossen
Voralpenseen", Stand: 04 / 2000), Bayerische Landesanstalt für Fischerei
http://www.nabu.de/nh/archiv/liste596.htm / http://www.greenpeace-magazin.de / (issue 1 /1997) /
From what I have read I am almost convinced that many conservationists understand that the situation has got out of hand. The problem is how to get out of the situation without losing face. The
solution everywhere will be that the laws won't be changed and that more licenses to protect fisheries will be granted. The conservationists will duly protest but that will be it. This, of course,
leaves the backdoor open to retake the initiative should the cormorant population drop drastically
again owing to non-protective causes like disease. It strikes me as a very strange idea to allow laser
guns to shy the birds away so they can do damage elsewhere. Yet another absurdity in this cormorant story is that the (theoretical) solution of the cormorant problem is achieved when the fish
stocks get so scarce that the number of cormorants will be reduced by shortage of fish. What then –
restocking the empty waters so that there can be more cormorants again? And finally there is the
hypothetical case that the almighty omnipresent cormorant actually destroys the living of other
water birds. An interesting thought because then there will be inevitable clashes between all those
high-minded and high-principled lovers of nature.

above all for obstructing cormorant and fish, the self-fulfilment of hunter and hunted. The anglers are, of course, the real culprits in the story:

> *Greedy anglers, not content with torturing and murdering fish, have now set their sights on cormorants as well. They have launched a campaign to have cormorants removed from the list of protected species. This gives anglers a free hand to shoot cormorants so that they don't interfere with their fishing ... All the cormorant is doing is feeding herself and her family while anglers catch fish for the sheer pleasure of it. Surely the cormorant's survival should be put above the pleasure of anglers?[165]*

I don't think any angler would contradict this if the cormorant was in any real danger. Yes, certainly, there can be instances when the pleasure of anglers must come second – but not on the basis of hysteria about millions of cormorants.

Very popular with valiant cormorant protectors is the argument that the cormorant thrives on different fish from those that are of interest to the angler. What a thing to say – all fish are of interest to the angler! But that is not really the nub. More pertinent is that the cormorant protectors obliquely accept the possibility of wiping out particular species of fish of "lesser value". By protecting the cormorant the way they do, the white knights for the black birds have to face that possibility. And if that should happen who will be prepared to accept responsibility? The cormorants? Most certainly not, as it was all the angler's fault from the very beginning...

Cast your mind back now to the noble philosophies of animal rights, animal liberation, non-interference, concepts of equal consideration and so on – and especially to cruelty. The cormorant scars a lot of big fish when it chases them. It has a go at them even though they're too big to gulp down. All it does is hurt them. The poor big fish then die painfully and by protecting the cormorant to the extent we have seen, great suffering is caused in the fish world. And doesn't the conservationist get great pleasure out of seeing the cormorants doing so well? Surely it's only because big fish don't yelp and whimper that otherwise decent people think it a good idea to sponsor and worship a bird causing so much suffering in the world of fish...

165 http://pisces.enviroweb.org/corm.html

Nature isn't what it used to be – there used to be a place in it for human beings before the Regans, Singers, Wilsons and Dawkins, to name but a few, abolished the good old-fashioned human being and replaced it with the humanimal[166] or the enlightened biomass. All those of you who still take yourselves to be human beings are simply an obstinate minority – discontinued models in evolutionary and philosophical terms. Just a matter of time … Anyway, especially among enlightened biomasses it is universal currency that nature can do no wrong. If as a humanimal you're an integral part of nature on a par with great apes and all other animals, then ethics is but a function of evolution.

In such a view humanimals can do whatever they please, it's neither right nor wrong. And with that the bottomless pit opens giving scientific, political and philosophical carte blanche to whatever atrocities humanimals are capable of. It opens the floodgates for an uninhibited, merciless social Darwinism in which there is no room for consideration for the weaker members of human society. Dawkins for one emphasises that nature is red in tooth and claw.[167] This being the case and you as fisherman being inescapably part of nature, you can do no wrong.

Luce thought this an inappropriate defence of angling because for a starter it's a godless defence and it characterises nature as cruel (red in tooth and claw) and a benevolent Creator couldn't have intended that. If somebody objects to your fishing and turns out to believe in evolution in as much as he takes human beings to be humanimals, I think it is a perfectly good defence to argue that your fishing is part of the evolutionary process. Since you are part of that nature which by definition can do no wrong, fishing can't be wrong. If nature isn't cruel I as fisherman can't be cruel. This holds the other way round too: if nature is cruel, I am cruel too because I am part of it. Something along those lines was probably in Sir Robert Bruce Lockhart's mind when he wrote:

I shall not attempt to defend the charge of cruelty. Nature is cruel and man is its child.[168]

The topic here is not cruelty but nature and man's place in it as

166 My word here, but I am certain somewhere out there in the real world there is a serious proposition that human beings should be called thus.
167 Richard Dawkins, *The Selfish Gene*, Oxford University Press (1999), p.2.
168 Sir Robert Bruce Lockhart, *My Rod My Comfort*, The Flyfisher's Classic Library, Ashburton, Devon, England (1999) p.17.

attributed or granted by animal rights and some environmentalist philosophers. Regan, Singer and others subscribe to a see-saw concept of nature. It's simple and very convenient. The "see" position is the one which understands man as a human being in the traditional sense with all his powers of deliberation. The "saw" position is characterised by the full fusion or re-integration of human beings into nature and the animal kingdom. The "saw" position is humanimal. On the whole we should spend 95% of our time as humanimalian vegans in the "saw" position, and only for granting animals rights and whatever should we push ourselves into the "see" position. This imaginary see-saw has only two states, up and down; it's a binary see-saw. The beauty of it is that you can effortlessly change from one position to the other according to what the issue is.

Functional to the core, and in this sense absolutist. It is precisely such philosophical structures which animal rights advocates and some environmentalists have managed to inculcate in parts of the public mind.

Nature isn't what it used to be – and the slightly overconfident attitude of some scientists and philosophers today giving themselves the air of having it sussed out once and for all, might be in for a few surprises. The present-day enthusiasm and optimism about the possibilities of genetics might at some future time be borne out. Maybe not quite the way today's scientists assume. Inventions and new technology have a knack of making their own way. Daguerreotype, for example, was one of the pioneering processes of photography. Its discovery prompted the following perspicacious comment by Edgar Allan Poe:

> The results of the invention cannot, even remotely, be seen – but all experience, in matters of philosophical discovery, teaches us that, in such discovery, it is the unforeseen upon which we must calculate most largely. It is a theorem almost demonstrated, that the consequences of any new scientific invention will, at the present day exceed, by very much, the wildest expectations of the most imaginative.[169]

Indeed what a way we've come from daguerreotype to the digital camera. Or from the Spirit of St. Louis to Concorde. Most likely events will take a completely unexpected turn anyway.

---

169 E.A Poe, "The Daguerreotype", http://xroads.virginia.edu/~HYPER/POE/daguer.html

Like the other day when I went with Jim to a lake in the mountains. Jim is my nephew and there is no doubt about his fishing gene. He has fished with me during his holidays since he was eight. The weather forecast that day called for a winter preview, as can happen at the beginning of September. On a day like that you're more likely to win the pools than stir a fin. I had suggested a day off – tying flies and putting all the gear back in ship-shape condition. Jim however was adamant – the lake it had to be.

Okay, I thought, this is going to be the didactic day. I told Jim that it was going to be a cold day but didn't assist him putting his clothes and gear together. He chose his light jacket. I packed in an extra shirt and a jumper – he was going to need them. Off we went and made it in time for the first cable car that morning. Jim had never been to that lake before and his excitement mounted as steadily as the cable car. He had a thousand and one questions and lost himself in a thousand and one speculations about the lake, the fish, the flies – he was babbling away enthusiastically like one of the clear mountain brooks we were going to meet on our way to the lake.

An instance of hunting fever fuelled by dreams of big trout. It is like that, isn't it? When you're on your way to fishing you can't help wondering what's going to happen that day. Some days you're pretty cool about it, on other days you lose yourself completely in the clouds of piscatorial reverie. The unpredictability of it is part of its essence. It's a variant of when you think about the future, about fate. Uncertainty provokes the wildest speculations. The only certain thing about the future is that it's going to happen one way or another. The uncertainty about it is probably the one single most striking demonstration of the limits of human power and nothing puts high-horsed scientists and philosophers better in their place than their absolute inability to predict the human – let alone the world's – fate at large. In contrast the fisherman knows that Fortuna[170] has her own mind. This does not in the least diminish the angler's enthusiasm. After all, she does smile now and then on the daydreaming angling optimist, trying even in adverse conditions, and then a big fish takes.

Anyway, the opening of the cable car's door was the starting gun for Jim. Like a sprinter he shot out of his starting blocks and ran straight into a wall of icy air. Just for a split second you could see a shadow of doubt passing his mind. Visibility was at the moment still fine but the clouds in the distance

170 Fortuna is the Roman Goddess of fate

looked, unlike the frilly beauties of imagination, menacingly real. The promised lake was a demanding hour's walk away. For me, that is, not for a teenager like Jim, bursting with energy and expectations. While I tried to find a steady rhythm for the steep bit he pranced around me like a puppy. He even walked backwards uphill, bombarding me with questions and a remark to the effect that old me should speed things up a bit. After all, we'd come here for fishing, not for hanging about.

On that day Jim could have tutored chamois. For a moment I feared he would suggest pushing me uphill, making me feel even older than I am. And as a sort of icing on the cake of the uphill part of the journey he spotted the marmots before I did.

Of course, although I inwardly pretended otherwise, Jim's cajoling made me walk faster than I intended. After the nasty bit was over there was a plain with scattered bushes and a lone pine tree and then followed an equally steep descent to the lake. By the time we reached the plain a vanguard mist had wrapped the scenery in wet, grey, cold. Of course there was nobody around except Jim, myself and, judging from the sound of the bells in the very far distance, some cows. Wafts of bad weather moved in on us. Pausing for breath, I watched Jim hopping in and out of visibility, envying him for a second for his youth, his diabolical fitness and light-heartedness. Before I could indulge in some futile, prematurely senile nostalgia, things began to happen. I was about to pass that lone weather- beaten pine tree when my mushroom stalker's nose picked up a weak signal… there was just the faintest of scents but no doubt in my mind.

With the demeanour of a priest about to perform a royal wedding ceremony, I approached the source of that scent. I yelled a profane and commanding "Ji …!" into the grey nothingness. He was, of course, beside me before the "m" had left my lips. There it was, and we stared at it dumbfounded like hypnotised rabbits. With that majestic immobility which is its perfect camouflage, it stood there waiting to be picked: the cep of all ceps.

It was big, very big, bigger than anything I had seen before. Four pounds maybe but what had us really spellbound was its beauty. It immediately made Jim forget about the fishing and there was no question of picking it immediately. After carefully checking the vicinity to see whether there were other ceps, we leaned our rod tubes on the pine tree and marvelled at the miracle from all sides. The proportions in terms of symmetry were such that you could have measured it in nanometres and wouldn't have found a fault. It was the sturdy type, wearing and supporting its cap comfortably. The cap was a wet, glistening bright brown with a dash of orange. Not a single pine needle had fallen on it, as if there was an aesthetic awareness somewhere that this cep was out of bounds for any distracting elements. The drawing of the white honeycomb network net was of such regularity it would have put any printing press to shame. Inspecting the beauty flat on our bellies, we could also see that there could not be a single worm in it – this was as pure a cep as you would ever get. The supreme sensation however, was the smell. As we had our noses very close to the ground, the olfactory appreciation included earthy elements with hints of cow dung, moss, freshly moistened granite and pine. The main aroma was of a rich, nutty complexion which really must be one of the smells of paradise. More down-to-earth, Jim's pragmatic suggestion was to pick it and then to press on for the lake.

This catapulted me into a didactic fit of lecturing. I was trying to impress on Jim the general idea that we were not locusts laying waste to whatever happened to be in our path. We human beings, I pontificated, were different. We can think in more than just the one dimension and in this case that would mean leaving the cep where it was and picking it on our way back. After all on a day like this when only mad dogs and Englishmen would venture outdoors, there would be nobody coming this way. Even if somebody did, he was unlikely to spot the cep because it couldn't be seen from the track. And more importantly, if we left the cep where it was now it would stay perfectly fresh. Jim didn't look convinced. I rambled on about short-term gains and the fast-buck mentality. Jim's eyes looked pleadingly heavenwards for help to stop the sermon. His prayers were answered by a short but incisively cold shower which induced a quick, authoritative decision to leave the cep where it was. Jim concurred, if only for the reason that we would finally get to the lake and down to business.

The fishing was, as I had expected, a complete non-event. Jim soldiered on bravely for hours, although even he must have soon realised there were no fish coming our way that day. Also he was probably feeling the cold on account of having taken the light jacket. His hands were getting numb. I offered him the shirt and the jumper but he wouldn't hear of it. Not to worry, walking back would warm him up again soon. So back we headed for the cep and the cable car station. What had been the nice bit down a couple of hours earlier was now the nasty bit up. But that cep up there beside that lone pine tree made the walk up that much easier. We would not return empty-handed.

It would be a great dinner party. The main course of Filet de cep, just gently heated in butter and seasoned with a little bit of salt and chives. Served with only plain white bread. That way the full flavour... mouth-watering thoughts and before my mind's eye I was already opening a bottle of Tariquet – would that be the wise choice?

Whatever, this cep would be even more than a culinary sensation. It would make the local newspaper, no doubt. Even the weather seemed to smile on the thought of that cep. There was a blue hole in the massive grey cloud allowing the sun to shine on the treasure. Another fifty metres to the plain. Jim as usual was way ahead of me. I happened to pause and look up the moment just before Jim reached the plain. Another ten steps or so and he would be able to see that lone pine tree in the distance. Still pausing I watched him suddenly stop as if struck by a bolt right out of the blue. He stood there, petrified, in a pose not unlike a pointer. What was he seeing up there that left him motionless and speechless? What was going on? A UFO maybe? I was up there in no time and what I saw also cut my breath. There in the distance a dozen or so huge cows were holding their siesta around that lone pine tree. And even as far away as we were, we could see that the biggest of them all sat exactly on the very spot. Tons of cow against two kilos of cep – there couldn't be much left of that beauty. Indeed there wasn't. After a little gentle prodding the monster cow agreed to get up, not without that typically bovine reproachful look, and what we saw was a true heart-breaker: squashed cep.

No fish, no cep, no lesson for Jim. At least not the one I had in mind. Plenty to ruminate for me. I felt ridiculous but at the same time I thought the whole situation outrageously funny. Jim saw it that way too and all of a sudden we couldn't help shaking with laughter. And for years to come Jim reminded me with, "Yes Alex, I know we're not locusts" when I was in danger of getting carried away.

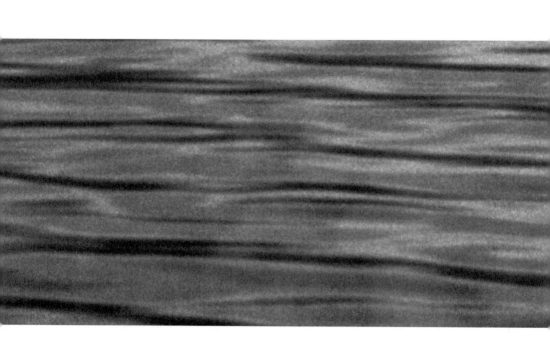

Chapter 7

SHORT CUT

Animal rights and anti-angling are about changing society. The marrow of the "cruelty-free" vegan state is totalitarian. The death of traditional ethics which Peter Singer welcomes opens, on the other hand, new horizons for infanticide and bestiality. The point to note is that the champion of animal liberation and anti-angling, while being very fussy about pain in a shrimp, allows the killing of perfectly healthy infants and sees in bestiality no offence to our status as human beings. Don't discuss angling next time you're challenged. Discuss the basis of anti-angling (remember there is no substance in the cruelty charge) which is

1. Anti-animal

Rights, whether moral or legal, entail duties. All else makes nonsense of rights. If rights are granted to animals, then animals as right holders, also have duties. Not only towards us but towards one another as well. This in turn means that the animal kingdom would have to convert to vegetarianism. As we have seen, radical vegetarians don't balk at trying to turn their cats into vegetarians. Animal rights is not only a perversion of the notion of rights but also a violent usurpation of the animal kingdom. Of nature. Of creation. It's pure megalomania.

2. Anti-culture

Animal rights or liberation is anti-Christian to the core. No compromise. Christianity is the basis of Western culture. We are not just talking moral values, we are talking about a way of life and above all about individual freedom. A "cruelty-free" dictatorship is the logical consequence of animal rights and animal liberation. Animal rights is totalitarian.

3. Anti-human

Deep down, the philosophies of Tom Regan, Peter Singer and other friends of animals and earth are anti-human in the sense that they tend to see human beings as an unfortunate complication in evolution. A regrettable defect. Their works don't emit any joy of life, they convey no meaning and no hope. There is, typically, no emotion in their philosophy. Bureaucrats. Merciless executioners.

Again, don't discuss angling. There's nothing wrong with it. Discuss, if anything, the basis of anti-angling.

Be a philosopher; but, amidst all your philosophy, be still a man![171]

Credit where credit is due: the animal rights and environmentalist movements deserve great credit for making the public more sensitive to vital issues such as the abuses in factory farming (also an environmental problem), the use of animals in research and, in general, of the relationship between man and beast. Equally valuable is the contribution the movement has made to the reawakening and remotivation of government agencies for animal protection and the protection of the environment. I repeat: great credit. Yet by fully recognising this it doesn't follow that you or I have to swallow the underlying philosophies and precepts hook, line and sinker. Not at all.

It's not quite clear how mankind arrives at granting animals the rights that are due to them. Nevertheless, once those rights are granted we will supposedly live in world peace and harmony. The nexus being that the humane treatment of animals also entails a change in inter-human relations. These are the vaguest of terms but that's all there is. Politically speaking Regan and Singer hold their cards very close to their chest (if there are cards at all). There is, for example, not a word (if there is I missed it) in *Animal Liberation*, in *Practical Ethics* or in *The Case for Animal Rights* about capitalism. The words capital and capitalism do not show in the index of these three books. This is very strange; it is at least of academic interest to know what economic system would be conducive to animal liberation. After all, capitalism is the economic environment in which all the poor animals of this world are supposedly so brutally trapped. Singer doesn't seem too keen to analyse the role of capitalism in animal suppression. This is fairly surprising because capitalism evolved out of a Christian background. There is a causal relation between the Christian religion and capitalism. There are those historians who still see substance in the Weberian thesis[172] of the link between Protestantism and capitalism. Others point emphatically to Renaissance Florence as the birthplace of modern capitalism. Either way the cultural climate was generated by Christianity.

171 David Hume, *Enquiries*, Oxford University Press, Third Edition (1975), p.9.
172 *Protestantism and the Rise of Capitalism* is available online at
http://xroads.virginia.edu/~hyper/WEBER/cover_old.html

Christianity, its values and history, we hear time and again from Singer and others, is the main source of animal oppression and suffering. Why not attack its economic basis just as violently as its spiritual values? "Cruelty-free" economics heralds the end of the free-market economy. The reason is as simple and obvious as can be: for moral reasons the vegan state couldn't tolerate animal products of any description. This means the state decides what's on the market and what is not. State intervention, state control, state everything – the implications of the "cruelty-free" economy are nothing short of totalitarian. What, for example, about fortunes derived from animal-based or related business – will they be confiscated? The totalitarian aspect probably explains the veil over the economic and political side of animal rights.

There is also complete silence about the implications of animal liberation for the organisation of society. Who, for example, polices compliance with the new animal laws? No problem: after mankind has been brain-washed (that is, genetically modified) all will be bliss between humanimals. The jobless police officers can form the NS, i.e. the Nutrition Squad,[173] to make sure predatory animals stick to their vegan diet. Regan and Singer are remarkably timid on the political and socio-economic front. Are Regan and Singer afraid to spell out the consequences of an implementation of their views? Would this alienate some of their establishment support? And are they, by omitting a sketch or revelation of their political ideas,[174] letting others do aimless dirty work? Are they instigators shying away from responsibility, washing their hands in innocence like in the case of the Inuit? Whatever the case, their political philosophy is vague to the point of non-existence. In all their glorious pretence, Singer and Regan fail to give us an idea of what the new moral world order, with animals liberated and rights being granted, will look like. The only thing that is certain is the dictate of reason. Their reason. That's not good enough. Especially not for the abolition of angling.

---

173 A term coined by David S. Oderberg in *Applied Ethics*, Blackwell, Oxford (2000), p.137.
174 There is a little book on political matters by Peter Singer titled *A Darwinian Left*, Yale University Press (2000). In his usual grandiosely self-confident and sweeping style he confines the Left to the mission of reducing pain and suffering in the world. The Left, contends Singer, has no other choice than to adopt utilitarianism and Darwinism as its guiding doctrines. On the program-matic side Singer would like the Left to "accept that there is such a thing as human nature, and to find out more about it, so that policies can be grounded on the best available evidence of what human beings are like." Best available evidence? What an opening for mad scientists and power-hungry politicians. Among many other things, including the pulling down of the species barrier, Singer wants also to "promote structures that foster cooperation rather than competition and attempt to channel competition into socially desirable ends". Socially desirable ends are nothing other than preferences and Singers's political philosophy in this tract boils down to the noncommit-tal glibness of simplistic lifestyle deliberations.

Remember, the villain of the piece is Christianity: Thomas Aquinas and friends. Being Christian is equivalent to being an animal abuser. Christianity stands in the way of harmony between man and animal. Christianity, according to Singer, is also the main obstacle to happy relationships with animals. Bestiality is no problem as long as there is no cruelty to the animal involved. Singer opines:

... sex with animals does not always involve cruelty.[175]

Then Singer excels himself in the concluding paragraph:

At a conference on great apes a few years ago, I spoke to a woman who had visited Camp Leakey, a rehabilitation center for captured orangutans in Borneo run by Birute Galdikas, sometimes referred to as "the Jane Goodall of orangutans" and the world's foremost authority on these great apes. At Camp Leakey, the orangutans are gradually acclimatised to the jungle, and as they get closer to complete independence, they are able to come and go as they please. While walking through the camp with Galdikas, my informant was suddenly seized by a large male orangutan, his intentions made obvious by his erect penis. Fighting off so powerful an animal was not an option, but Galdikas called to her companion not to be concerned, because the orangutan would not harm her, and adding, as further reassurance, that "they have a very small penis." As it happened, the orangutan lost interest before penetration took place, but the aspect of the story that struck me most forcefully was that in the eyes of someone who has lived much of her life with orangutans, to be seen by one of them as an object of sexual interest is not a cause for shock or horror. The potential violence of the orangutan's come-on may have been disturbing, but the fact that it was an orangutan making the advances was not.

That may be because Galdikas understands very well that we are animals, indeed more specifically, we are great apes. This does not make sex across the species barrier normal, or natural, whatever those much-misused words may mean, but it does imply that it ceases to be an offence to our status and dignity as human beings.[176]

Speak for yourself!

175 http://www.nerve.com/Opinions/Singer/heavyPetting
176 http://www.nerve.com/Opinions/Singer/heavyPetting

Singer's stand on bestiality as outlined above reveals that he does not care about either human beings or animals. From an animal rights point of view bestiality is the grossest violation of principle possible. In the individual case it is an assault on the animal in question and generally the extension of the human dominion robs animals of their autonomy. If ever there was speciesism, this surely is it! And how does it "follow" from this incident that bestiality ceases to be an offence to human dignity? What sort of reasoning is that? Doesn't it rather follow, with babies and children in Singer's view being on a par with animals, that paedophilia is just as blameless as bestiality? Next in line is surely a carte blanche for paedophilia.

Singer's moral philosophy, if it can be thus called, is unable to commit itself to saying that such and such is wrong. On the other hand everything, except eating meat[177], is permissible: infanticide, euthanasia, bestiality – you name it. With a bit of good will and clever reasoning you'll be able to justify anything on the basis of preferences. There are no moral values or principles in this philosophy. Nor is there compassion or any joy of life. It's an abysmal black hole devoid of any humanness. (Professor Singer teaches at the "Center for Human Values" at Princeton University).

When the "Father of Animal Rights" has spoken, activists are quick off the mark translating the philosophical teachings into reality: Love-ins in zoos? Here is what the president of PETA thinks:

The president of PETA agrees with Singer's beliefs about animals. She said the following about his article which appeared on nerve.com. "It's daring and honest, and it does not do what some people read into it, which is condone any violent acts involving an animal, sexual or otherwise."

When asked how an animal can consent to sex, she said, "It sounds like [your question] is an attempt to make this so narrow and so unintellectual in its focus. You know, Peter Singer is an intellectual, and he looks at all nuances of an issue, the whole concept of consent with animals is very different."[178]

Forget all about it but don't forget that anti-angling and anti-hunting for that matter are based on the views of people who seriously think that

---

177 In most if not all cases. Singerian ethics are open to anything. If animals are painlessly raised and slaughtered, it is OK to eat them.
178 http://www.massnews.com/601ed.htm

infanticide is a great idea and bestiality potentially great fun. It is at this level that anti-angling should be taken on! There is no point in defending angling in angling-terms since the debate is not about fish or fishing but about fundamental values. Angling has come under fire because of animal rights ideas not because of cruelty or whatever else is said against angling. In contemporary anti-angling and anti-hunting propaganda, the claim of alleged cruelty is but a means to an end: the abolition of angling is a stage on the way to a cruelty–free society. Anti-angling is about you, not fish.

Over the past few decades the arguments against angling have changed from the specific cruelty level to a more general discussion about values. There has also been a significant change in numbers: while not all animal rights supporters are permanently engaged in anti-angling activities, they can be mobilised at the right moment. Those who take themselves to be animal liberators will rally behind any cause in need of temporary support in crucial moments! Animal rights unite the most diverse interests and collectively are a force to be reckoned with. It's like football: A staunch Rangers supporter has no emotional or rational problems in wholeheartedly supporting a Scotland side in which there are also players of the arch-rivals Celtic.

One practical consequence for the angler could be a change of attitude towards charities which ostensibly support animal or environmental causes. Next time you're tempted to contribute, check out the charity's stand on animal rights. If it supports rights, don't contribute, if it's welfare, do as you please. Don't accept any waffling: if they are not sure what they're on about, forget it. In fact the angling clubs and associations should publish a list that animal welfare or environmental anglers should support. Those deemed worthy of support should then be monitored – just to be on the safe side.

Don't discuss angling, ask questions about animal rights!!! Point to its misanthropy, which is an enemy of all culture and life. The concept of animal rights is, however diluted, the source and inspiration for those nice people who want you to reel up now. For ever. Misanthropic – that's surely exaggerated. Or is it? "All is number" we have heard from Pythagoras; "All is rights", Regan might say; and for Singer it could be "All is preferences". Three reason-drunk philosophers failing to grasp or refusing to see that being human involves more than biology, numbers, rights and logic. The bio-logic-only, blinkered view of the world just misses out on such strange and beautifully irrational things as love, compassion, kindness, faith or the simple joy of being alive. When I said that Regan's and Singer's philosophies are misanthropic, then it was also on the grounds that, for whatever reason, they systematically ignore human sentiments. These are at least just as important as reason and logic but they don't come into play at all. On the contrary. This is what Regan has to say about wildlife management, the task of which is to defend animals' rights:

> *We owe this to wild animals, not out of kindness, nor because we are against cruelty, but out of respect for their rights.*[179]

The abolition of culture and sentiment in man and morals, to which both Singer and Regan obviously subscribe, turns them into philosophical machines reasoning their way heartlessly and inexorably from A to B. Philosophers undoubtedly they are.

179 Tom Regan, *The Case for Animal Rights*, University of California Press, Berkeley and Los Angeles CA (1985), p.357.

Chapter 8

SHORT CUT

Anti-anglers are, as we have seen, not really interested in fish at all. Anglers are, and that is why there are still fish in rivers and lakes. Aesthetics is a branch of philosophy dealing with questions of beauty in nature and art and how beauty affects us. A pike is a beautiful being. Fishing for pike thus could be the quest for beauty.

One of the pleasures of angling is the hope of experiencing something extraordinary, something beautiful, something sublime. Rod and line are, in Wordsworth's words, the

> True symbol of the foolishness of hope,
> Which with its strong enchantment led us on
> By rocks and pools, shut out from every star
> All the green summer, to forlorn cascades
> Among the windings of the mountain brooks
> Unfading recollections! ...

This is the romantic version. And there is also the match fisher's hope for success on the big day. All anglers are looking for something – beauty of some sort. All fishing has this aspect in it which has to be cultivated in order to raise the standard of the sport and its overall acceptance. Much has been done in terms of educating young anglers, and – more still needs to be done. First and foremost the ditches between the different types of angling have to be filled. Remember: if one type of angling is wrong, so are all the others!

There is pleasure in all types of angling. This pleasure is in every respect legitimate, for there is no cruelty involved. The point to take on board is that even though this is so, animal rightists still insist that fishing should be banned. Animal rightists and anti-anglers are not interested in the "suffering" fish or the hunted animal, they are interested in the values and the way of life of fishermen and hunters – and they want those eradicated. Make no mistake, that is what the compassion of animal rightists is all about.

A question linked to ethics is why men go fishing. There are not sufficient rational grounds to explain the addictive nature of angling. There is only one real answer to that: fish and find out!

The beauty of angling

That fish do not experience pain and suffering doesn't let anglers off the hook. Quite the contrary! James Rose concludes his article *"The Neurobehavioral Nature of Fishes and the Question of Awareness and Pain"* aptly:

> *Although it is concluded from the foregoing analysis that the experiences of pain and emotional distress are not within the capacity of fishes, this conclusion in no way devalues fishes or diminishes our responsibility for respectful and responsible stewardship. Fishes constitute a highly evolved, diverse and complex life form whose history on the Earth vastly eclipses the brief existence of humans. Our diverse uses of fishes have ancient historical precedents and modern justifications, but our increasingly deleterious impacts on fishes at the population and ecological levels require us to use our best scientific knowledge and understanding to foster their health and viability.* [180]

In what follows I can, of course, only talk from personal experience. The first topic I want to mention, believe it or not, is litter. Incredibly enough this seems still to be a problem although the angling press, clubs and associations have done a lot to inform the angling public. From my experience this is one of the truly classless phenomena of this world – whether on a one, ten or a hundred-pound-a-day fishery you're still bound to find, worst of all, discarded line. In my fishing jacket there is one pocket reserved for disused line – it's so simple and you won't be haunted by pictures of entangled birds. Of course, I surely have accidentally lost or forgotten some line sometime – nobody's perfect – but every fisherman should make a real effort. The same goes for all other stuff. Littering banks or boats with cans, paper, cigarette stubs and food leftovers is, apart from being most impolite to your fellow angler, an aesthetically unpardonable sin. Fishing has an aesthetic side which is integral to the experience. Now *there* is a real problem. Let me explain.

It was a late Sunday afternoon in summer. The sun was getting ready to set. I was preparing myself for another hour or two of fishing in an atmosphere which Lord Byron captured perfectly with the following words:

180 *Reviews in Fisheries Science* 10(1): 1-38, CRC Press LLC (2002), p.33.

Mortal! To thy bidding bow'd,
From my mansion in the cloud,
Which the breath of twilight builds,
And the summer sunset gilds
With the azure and vermilion
Which is mixe'd for my pavilion;
Though thy quest may be forbidden
On a star beam I have ridden,
To thine adjuration bow'd;
Mortal – be thy wish avowe'd![181]

The conditions looked promising and there was a tickling presentiment of great things to come. Sometimes fish have a deep understanding of the aesthetic urge in an angler. They take at exactly the moment when you think "Now it would be beauty itself if a fish took". It happens. Sometimes. Anyway, there I was sitting concentrating intently in my boat, watching the tip of my rod (I was after whitefish), when all of a sudden I felt there was something very wrong. I looked around: nothing unusual. Still, there was something ... I turned fully round to check behind me and as I gazed at the sun I saw, believe it or not, hundreds of balloons about ready to land on me. They were in all colours – blue, red, green, purple, yellow – all amplified in intensity by the sunset light. All of them carried, attached on a string, a postcard saying that so-and-so had married that day, that this was part of a balloon-flying-competition and would the finder please etc. The balloons gently touched down on the lake and in the boat with a pinpoint accuracy, just as if they were fitted with some homing device. There I sat immersed in hundreds of seemingly fluorescent balloons. I felt positively silly. Would you be able to re-focus your attention immersed in balloons? And wouldn't you think it rather out of place to land a fish in such peculiar circumstances?

Why? Surely, it doesn't bother the whitefish the least bit if it's netted among balloons. That is probably so, but like cruelty the story of beauty is probably all in the mind. Beauty shapes angling experiences. Poetry and lore capture the spirit of angling, intensify the interest and point to zones beyond the mere catching of fish.

---

181 This is from "Manfred" and apart from its poetic merit I have chosen it because the events I tell here took place on Lake Thun, Switzerland. It is most likely that Lord Byron wrote those lines while staying in the Lake Thun region. For the full text see: www.bartleby.com/18/6

The scene is off St. Joseph's Island in the Amirantes. We're on board the *Cookie Two* with Skipper André and the deckhands Michael and Basil. My friend and guide Roland Henrion and I have just returned with the dinghy from fishing the flats there, an experience of a lifetime. Roland explains to me that on the way back we're going to try for sailfish. The theory is that behind the boat we're trailing lures without hooks: the teasers. With luck they will interest and raise a sailfish. When the sail is showing the lures are retrieved – the sailfish is teased in. Once it is within casting range the teasers are speedily brought in and the angler casts his fly in front of the sailfish. The hope is that the sailfish will duly take it.

The drill is straightforward. Whoever spots the sailfish warns the others by shouting, "Sail, sail!". Roland then takes over and commands the teasing operation. The next order is "Fly in the water!" to the angler and a couple of seconds later comes the all decisive "Cast!". Simultaneously the skipper goes into neutral. After the cast the angler works his fly with a few jerks so as to induce a take by the sailfish. Should it oblige, you have to wait a couple of seconds before you strike until the sailfish turns away with the fly. The exact time lapse is to think or say slowly and with respect, "God save the Queen" or if you're republican "God save Mister President".

That's the theory: in practice it's a bit more tricky. The casting can be quite demanding on a choppy sea – if you're lucky you can try twice but the general rule is that your first cast is your only real chance. Then there is the time factor: you can cruise for days on end without even getting anywhere near a sailfish. The choice of fly (pattern and size) is, under such circumstances, much more than a rational deliberation. In the end it's an act of faith. Like in real life, if all goes well, all is well. Should you however raise a sail and it ignores the fly – there will be a lot of "if" reasonings going on. The final decision regarding the choice of fly is yours. There is no doubt about that. The guide, however, will tell you what he would put on based on his experience. On principle I always opt for something completely different, not least because Roland will then, ever so slightly annoyed, explain to me why the other fly would have been the better one. I have learned a lot from him in this way.

Back to the *Cookie Two*. On that day Roland was satisfied that I had understood everything so off we went. I sat on the rail looking back at St. Joseph, the palm tree line and the vast pristine flats where we had spent a couple of hours of the most glorious fishing there is. In the end I actually didn't fish that much because the flats on St. Joseph must be one of the world's most beautiful spots. The colours, the light, the life and the loneliness were of such power that I stood there mouth agape watching what was happening around me. Occasionally casting a line but always distracted by something or other: a ray passing in majestic style, in the distance the splash of barracudas chasing baitfish, a curious baby shark circling around me, some bird shouting "Sail, sail!". "That wasn't a bird," I thought. Indeed it wasn't. It was Roland and the entire crew trying to yank me out of my daydreams. Hazily I came round, spotted the sail and on the command "Fly in the water" I produced the most awful and untimely cast ever – the angling world hasn't seen the like of it before or since. Fully awake shortly afterwards, I realised that I had screwed it up. If looks could kill I would have been dead on the spot.

With a sigh that could be heard a hundred miles away, the skipper cranked the gear in. To the utter amazement of all, seconds later the sailfish reappeared. This time round, no mistake. It was beautifully teased in, my cast was as precise and sweet as you can get it and the sailfish took. But in all the excitement I forgot about "God save the Queen". In great style I pulled the fly right out of the sailfish's mouth. After temporary petrification, the atmosphere on the Cookie Two changed to glacial, which was just as well because after all it was a very hot day. The thawing took a couple of hours, everybody avoiding direct eye contact. These are the great tests of friendship.

When I told Jim the story of how stupidly I'd missed that sailfish off St. Joseph there wasn't just amusement in his eyes – there was a flicker of yearning and excitement there. The point is that fishing tales, like poems, will be with us for as long as they fire off the reader's or the listener's imagination and sense of beauty. As long as there is that sort of sentiment around there will be anglers trying their luck – unless, of course, angling is abolished on the grounds discussed above. But back to the beauty of angling.

Discarded line, apart from being potentially harmful, is an insult to that sense of beauty that accompanies angling. The same applies to littered boats or river or lake banks. In fact anglers should strive to leave boat, lake or the bank cleaner than they found them (it's not just anglers who dump rubbish on river banks). It might be said now that this sort of visual pollution is peanuts in comparison with, say, the non-visible pollution of water going on at large. This may be true but the point is that anglers who cares about small-scale pollution will also fight large-scale pollution if they can. But there is, environment apart, an equally strong consideration: aesthetics. The sight of a dead stream is an insult to everybody's sense of beauty. The running water is just running water – there is no longer that happy babbling, full of life and surprises. All its beauty is gone and filling the onlooker with a profound sense of dejection. The fight against pollution of any kind is also a fight for beauty.

Here is a striking example showing how a sense of beauty can determine your actions. The context is that of an angler who has caught his first salmon:

> *I can still see that salmon lying, glistening silver and blue, on the thwart of the boat I had used to cross the river in order to fish the pool. I was so overcome with emotion that I found it impossible to continue fishing: all the co-ordination needed to cast had gone. I walked down the river trying to compose myself with the help of several cigarettes, before returning to the boat to make sure that the fish was there and the whole episode had not merely been a dream. This supreme occasion, the ultimate in fishing, was tarnished when I returned to the boat after more perambulations, and noticed blood seeping from a wound halfway along the fish's side, where the gaff had penetrated the flesh before lifting it out of the water. The wound offensively interrupted the magnificent streamlined shape of a powerful ten-pound fish. I repeatedly washed and bathed the fish in the river, hoping the scar would heal and it would be restored to its former glory. It seemed such an unfitting end to a creature which filled me with nothing but admiration. I promised that salmon that I would never, whatever the circumstances, use a gaff again. I have kept my promise over the years, preferring to use a net or a tailer which prevents any damage to a fish while it is being landed and leaves the majestic salmon to lie with elegance and dignity, even in death.[182]*

Beauty does come into the ethics of angling more than one would think. The gaff here is banned for aesthetic reasons – none other! If you look at another aspect such as barbless hooks, the same considerations come into play. Barbless hooks are mandatory for the simple reason that the actual

---

182 Geoffrey A. Smith, *Reflections of a Fisherman*, Souvenir Press, London (1987), p.6.

handling (if any at all) of fish is that much easier. Barbed hooks sometimes get so awkwardly stuck that it is virtually impossible to take the hook out without seriously injuring the fish, thereby drastically diminishing its chances for survival. The fish will vainly attempt to dive, swim in a circle or dart about just below the surface – it is not an aesthetically satisfying sight to see a badly injured fish dying, whatever the cause! If on the other hand you want to keep the fish, you kill it first and then remove the hook. Here again barbless hooks are much better than barbed ones. You can ease the hook out just like that – no need to hold the fish and apply pressure. When fishing for whitefish, for example, this is of great value because pressure diminishes the quality of whitefish meat. A fish handled badly owing to the use of a barbed hook is not part of the beauty of angling.

The Garonne Man

It was early spring and I had some business in Toulouse in the South of France. A most beautiful, friendly, historically important city on the River Garonne. You might also be interested to learn that the magnificent Church of the Jacobins there happens to be the final resting place of St. Thomas Aquinas. On the bank of the Garonne I sat enjoying the sun.

A fisherman rode his bike along the bank. He settled for a spot not far from me and had, of course, my undivided attention for various reasons. To begin with I noticed he didn't have a landing net. Nor, apart from the fishing rod, any other obvious gear or garment indicating fishing. Out of the pocket of his jacket came a piece of bread. A fairly long rod, a very light float and judging by the amount of bread he moulded on the end, a tiny hook. What followed was a great display of angling skill. The fish the man was after were five to seven centimetres long. Their take was incredibly quick but our man was sharp. He didn't miss one – I would have got maybe one in ten. On top of that he seemed to know exactly how they moved. If he hadn't an offer for two or three runs he adjusted his cast to a bit further out or in. He caught maybe a dozen fish in this manner and then moved to a spot further down the river where he repeated the performance. For all I knew he did this every day. The point is, of course, that he put all those fish back in again. They were caught for no other purpose than being caught. This was the archetypal catch-and-release fisherman – and no discussion about ethics and angling can afford not to address this topic, although seas of ink or toner or whatever have already been used up in polemic and in search of wisdom.

The cruelty question seems to be once more at centre stage. We discussed cruelty and concluded that where there is no pain and suffering there can be no cruelty. Cruelty can't be an issue in the classical angling sequence of catch – kill – eat. Nor can it be in catch-and-release. What comes into play there is the stress response caused in fish and their subsequent chances of survival. Stress, like pain and suffering, must not be viewed in human terms. What is discussed here is not cruelty or an emotionally unpleasant experience for fish but the question: in what way can sense be made of catching a fish in order to release it?

169

There is agreement about the facts of the situation as to what happens when a fish is being played. It's all about the building up of lactic acid. Dr. Bruno Broughton explains:

The muscles involved are of two main types. The bulk of a fish's body is composed of so-called white muscle, while the much smaller areas at the roots of the fins and in a strip along the centre of each flank comprise red muscle. The red muscle receives a good supply of blood and contains ample quantities of fat and glycogen, the storage form of glucose, which is used for most routine, day-to-day swimming movements. In contrast, the white muscle has a poor blood supply and few energy stores, and it is used largely for short term, fast swimming.

It might seem odd that the body of an animal adapted so efficiently to its environment should be composed almost entirely of a type of muscle it rarely uses. However, this huge auxiliary power pack carried by a fish is of crucial significance if the life of the fish is threatened – by a predator, for instance – because it enables the fish to swim rapidly away from danger. But the use of white muscle by a fish does have a knock-on effect on the fish's internal body processes. Because of the poor blood system to the white muscle, these tissues receive little oxygen. When they are being used for prolonged periods, the energy stored within them cannot be 'burnt off' properly and an intermediate chemical, lactic acid, is produced. Since this substance is acidic, it can cause internal problems unless it is converted to harmless end products.

When the fish ceases using its white muscle, the lactic acid moves by diffusion to the red muscle, where the oxygen in the blood supply can burn it off completely. In the meantime, the fish suffers from an "oxygen debt" which it must repay as soon as possible.

As most unfit people will testify, a similar situation occurs in humans when they run for a bus, say. Afterwards, heavy panting may occur, during which the body takes enough air to pay off the body's oxygen debt and break down the lactic acid formed in the muscles.

There are, however, major differences between people and fish in the speed with which this reaction takes place. In human beings panting may last for several minutes; in fish the equivalent process may last for several hours. During that time, the metabolism of the fish has to cope with the influx of lactic acid and, in severe circumstances, this may upset the internal chemistry of the fish to such an extent that its life is at risk. [183]

183 http://www.anglersnet.co.uk/authors/bruno08.htm

It follows that the lower the exertion, the higher the chances of survival. This is why all anglers advocating catch-and-release stress the importance of the shortest possible playing time. This in turn means using the heaviest gear possible for the fish you're aiming to catch (line strength). Our man in Toulouse did everything right – the fish were so small, they were pulled out in a second and in another second they were swimming in the Garonne again. I doubt whether they had time at all to build up any of that lactic acid. But bigger fish are different: they put up a fight for dear life building up lactic acid and will have a more or less rough time recovering from being caught and handled. That much is, I believe, undisputed.

The mortality rate is where figures and opinions differ. How successful catch-and-release really is in an overall sense can't be assessed. Regionally and in species specific terms there can be reliable information, but not on a general level. The facts for carp are different from the facts for salmon and those in turn won't be the same for perch. On top of that, water temperature and water level on the day in question might also influence the successful practice of catch-and-release. Mortality rates after release differ widely between 1% and 43%. That, of course, is the crux. And in the term "mortality rate" there is the possibility of a long drawn-out death. Not all fish fatally weakened by the struggle with the angler and thereafter released find a mercifully quick end with the help of a pike, a seagull or another predator. Most will, though.[184]

The question we must address here is of a fundamental nature: does catch-and-release make sense, is it meaningful and, above all, is it ethical fishing? It could be argued, as it often is, that to exhaust a fish for the sake of playing it is pointless. Even our man on the Garonne might lose his touch for a couple of minutes, thereby wantonly injuring a couple of fingerlings and causing some untimely deaths. There seems to be a problem with the Garonne man's fishing because the fish he catches with almost mechanical precision are living beings. They are not highly sophisticated robot toy fish which feel and behave like real fish and which you can catch time and again.

184 The sources for this paragraph are:
Bryn Hammond, *Halcyon Days*, Swan Hill Press, Shrewsbury (1992). Chapter 11.
http://www.catchandreleasefound.org/release.html / http://www.nesportsman.com/articles/
article60.shtml /, http://www.seagrant.wisc.edu/greatlakesfish/catch.html
http://www.petaonline.org/liv/animaltimes/a299/fish.html
http://www.texs.com/bass_mortality_study/study.htm
http://espn.com/outdoors/conservation/s/c_fea_hooking_mortality.html
http://www.nesportsman.com/article59.shtml#to do

Indeed, if they were toy robots, the Garonne Man would give up immediately, saying that they weren't the real thing. Only if it's real fish you're after is it fishing – they've got to be living, otherwise there's no point. Hunters aren't satisfied with target shooting either – it's nothing like being out there stalking your prey. The object of the exercise is the hunt for an animal and even if what the Garonne man does looks like no such thing, the hunt must however remotely be present there.

The same incidentally applies to competition fishing – it's structurally the same problem as that of the Garonne man. Competition fishing seems the very antithesis of the bucolic tranquillity associated with all kinds of fishing known from literature and poetry. In fact, to many lone coarse and fly fishermen who hunt in solitude, the Garonne man and competition fishing wouldn't qualify as fishing at all. Let's scrutinise this. When I plan to catch perch for a filet de perche dinner I specifically choose tackle, bait, time, place etc. accordingly. While I'm fishing for perch, other fish like roach might take – these I put back because they don't fit the menu. In the case of my filets de perche I intend to keep the perch for eating (should I indeed catch any). There are a lot of pleasures involved in the process culminating in a great dinner. The Garonne man's and the competition fisher's intentions, methods and pleasures are obviously different – and different they may be, but that doesn't make their sport in any way morally inferior to mine. The pleasures involved derive basically from the same kind of pursuit: it's all angling and as such its morality needn't be questioned any more. Of course there can and will be discussions over tactics but that doesn't touch the fundamentals of angling. The issue of catch-and-release plays into all types of fishing, as Bryn Hammond points out:

Long before angling degenerated into the rigid divisions of game and coarse fishing, men would catch-and-release 'unwanted' species without any specific thoughts of the superiority of one species of fish over another.[185]

There is a real angler talking and a glimpse of wisdom hidden in these few words. As much as I admire Luce, he really did dodge the question of coarse fishing and I couldn't agree less with the following:

185 Bryn Hammond, *Halcyon Days*, Swan Hill Press, Shrewsbury (1992), p.105.

172

That the edibility of the fish has much to say to the morality of angling for them is confirmed by one's instinctive reactions to the capture of pike and perch. A self-observant angler is bound to notice how differently he feels towards them. He cannot help catching them at times when trolling; but they are a nuisance to him in more ways than one; they are a psychological nuisance to him when he sees them lying dead on the floor-boards; they offend his eye; they are 'kills'; but they are not what he came to get; they are not the proper objects of his angling. Pike and perch, of course, are not absolutely uneatable; but few sportsmen eat them. They have better fish to fry.[186]

I wish I could invite him round for some *filet de pérche* and *quenelles de brochet*.[187] Apart from that, what beautiful fish they are, and the hunt for pike and perch – with the fly or with conventional methods – is as challenging and demanding as it is exciting. The coarse and the game fisher are in the same boat not only on the cruelty issue, but also on the question of catch-and-release. The principles involved are the same. The action differs in as much as the salmon fisherman releases the salmon immediately whereas the competition fisher keeps his catch until the weigh-in after which the fish are released. catch-and-release seems to me a perfectly good idea which cannot, however, be universalised. There might be places where a strict catch-and-release policy is the right thing whereas in others it certainly isn't. It really all depends on circumstances and on skilful and educated anglers.

The Garonne man problem – i.e. does it make sense to catch fish for the sake of catching them – can't be solved by reference to catch-and-release per se, because it is an integral part of any fishing. We must therefore refocus on the situation where catch-and-release is the consciously chosen policy. The answer to the problem can only be found within the angler. Pleasure is the key word. The word "pleasure" will make not a few philosophers and probably some churchmen sit bolt upright. The reason for this intellectual and moral red alert is called Epicurus (341–270 BC) who discovered the value of pleasure for philosophy and made it the precondition of a morally good life:

186 A.A. Luce, *Fishing and Thinking*, Swan Hill Press, Shrewsbury, England (1990), p.184.
187 Escoffier lists over 15 different recipes for pike. There are also recipes for barbel, bream, dace and other freshwater fish which are not any more regarded worth eating. Convenience, lack of know-how, perceived lack of time and cheaper sea fish are presumably the main reasons. A comparison of cookery books illustrates the decline in culinary appreciation of freshwater fish: there were 66 recipes for 23 freshwater species and 5 recipes for 3 saltwater species in 1805. In 1933 it was 32 recipes for 10 freshwater species and 39 recipes for 18 saltwater species. Source: G. Wiegelmann and A. Mauss in *Fishing Cultures of the World*, ed. B. Gunda, Akadémiai Kiadó Budapest (1984), Vol.1, p.329.

It is impossible to live a pleasant life without living wisely and honorably and justly, and it is impossible to live wisely and honorably and justly without living pleasantly. Whenever anyone of these is lacking, when for instance, the man is not able to live wisely, though he lives honorably and justly, it is impossible for him to live a pleasant live.[188]

That sounds like sweet reason itself but in certain quarters it has caused uproar. To this very day few people, unless they are Epicureans, think of pleasure spontaneously as one virtue among others like humility, patience or charity – let alone the supreme moral good. This in itself was eyed with suspicion and together with Epicurus' atomistic view of the world in which the soul dies with the body, it was too much for some, for it is a thoroughly secular philosophy.

Through the centuries Epicurus had many admirers but on the whole he got a bad press or was ignored. The concept of pleasure then surfaced again prominently with utilitarianism in the form of:

...pleasure and the freedom from pain are the only things desirable as ends.[189]

John Stuart Mill then added preventively:

Now such a theory of life excites in many minds, and among them in some of the most estimable in feeling and purpose, inveterate dislike. To suppose that life has (as they express it) no higher end than pleasure – no better and nobler object of desire and pursuit – they designate as utterly mean and grovelling; as a doctrine worthy only of swine, to whom the followers of Epicurus were, at a very early period, contemptuously likened; and modern holders of the doctrine are occasionally made the subject of equally polite comparisons by its German, French and English assailants. When thus attacked, the Epicureans have always answered, that it is not they, but their accusers, who represent human nature in a degrading light; since the accusation supposes human beings to be capable of no pleasures except those of which swine are capable.[190]

This highlights the problem of pleasure but it still doesn't answer yet our question about the Garonne man. Pleasures come in all shapes and guises

---

188 http://www.atomic-swerve.net/tpg/index.html
189 John Stuart Mill, *Utilitarianism*, Collins/Fontana, Glasgow (1962), p.257.
190 Ibid., p. 258.

and in all degrees of intensity, and the nature of them varies greatly from the purely sensual to the purely intellectual.

As we have seen, the nature and pleasure of angling can't consist in inflicting pain and suffering on fish. The source of pleasure for the angler is definitely not pain and suffering and with that the whole anti-angling construct collapses. Or does it? No, it wouldn't, because the pleasure of going angling itself is the issue, say the anti-anglers, confirming that anti-angling is not so much about fish as about a conception of the world. Even if there is no pain and suffering involved, angling is still wrong because you interfere in an illegitimate way with nature. The dogma is that it is morally wrong to interfere with nature's ways. After the abolition of hunting and fishing, mushroom stalking is next in line. It is an off-the-beaten-track pursuit. It means, among other things, you accept that by stepping on dead leaves you cause an incredible amount of suffering and death among the countless little creatures that live in this beautiful universe of the forest floor. Like in a drop of water, the life underneath the leaves is of unbelievable richness. Think of the birds you startle, the deer you disturb, the trees you frighten – as a man and a mushroom stalker you're a nuisance for this world. If on top of that you forcefully evict a little worm or two from a cep – well, you qualify certainly for purgatory, if I am allowed to use that term. Anyway, the pleasure of mushroom stalking, just like the pleasure of angling, involves contact with nature – the wrong kind.

By the same reasoning, all sorts of horse or pony riding are out of the question. For a start any kind of riding qualifies in the animal rightists' books as torture and abuse. A cross-country ride will inevitably cause great suffering by the hoofs crushing all sorts of tiny animals. Any country pursuit really qualifies as criminal. What the right kind of contact or involvement with nature would be, is difficult to work out because there is no uniform code issued by animal rights advocates, fundamentalist vegetarians and radical environmentalists. It's all a bit misty and mystifying but one thing is certain: there is no place for hunting, fishing, mushroom stalking or horse riding in a world regulated by benevolent concern for animals and nature. What is required from hunters, fishermen, mushroom stalkers and horse riders is to do without the pleasures derived from intercourse with nature. And on the positive side they're asked to conform to the tenets of veganism and what-not. Again, and this can't be emphasised enough, anti-angling is not about fish. It's about what you should think about the world, how you should live and what you should or should not enjoy.

Somewhere in the vast spectre of pleasures the Garonne man takes pleasure in his catch-and-release fishing. He supposes (as I do) that all fishing is fundamentally okay and not cruel. But even so, does his pleasure warrant the potential loss of a fish life? For the anti-angler there is no question in the first place. Non-anglers, even those who are not anti-anglers, might be puzzled by the idea of catching fish and then letting them go, and some anglers would disapprove of it as a pointless exercise. And there is always the possibility of legislation: catch-and-release could be banned just like keepnets have been banned from some waters. But are the people mentioned and the legislators really the people that matter? Isn't it rather the case that the Garonne man's conscience should have the last say in the matter? If he looks deep, deep down into his conscience, his sense of aesthetics, his pleasure requirements, his ichthyological facts, his experience, his beliefs, his reason, his knowledge of possible objections, his feelings, his expertise and his awareness of the rules that govern the fishing on the Garonne and if he finds nothing, no reason, no moral sentiment that tells him not to fish like he fishes, then the matter is morally settled and he can enjoy his angling by accepting that in the course of it he might cause the death of some fish. The same applies to competition fishing. It's a matter of conscience, aesthetics and pleasure.

The answer to the original question "Does the Garonne man's pleasure , based on catch-and-release warrant the potential loss of a fish life?" is an unequivocal yes and comes in two stages. Stage one is a yes because there is nothing wrong with fishing as such. Stage two, the catch-and-release, is also a yes based on the Garonne man's conscience. This in turn also answers the question of "Does it make sense?". Yes, it does make sense to the Garonne man. Angling the way he does gives pleasure to the Garonne man and pleasure is good. The fact that it might not make sense to other people doesn't give them moral authority or superiority to judge him by saying he shouldn't fish the way he does.

Many philosophers including Singer, of course, probably regard conscience as old hat, a Christian relic not ethically relevant because listening to that inner voice

is more likely to be a product of one's upbringing and education than a source of genuine ethical insight.[191]

191 Peter Singer, *Practical Ethics*, pp.292–295.

This might be true as long as the soul searching is purely self-referential. If however conscience beats the system, so to speak, as it does in the case of conscientious objectors to military service, then its range widens dramatically. By the very nature of the subject (military service), conscience steps over the boundary of subjectivism. An enlightened search for the moral decision in one's conscience is not easy – especially if you make an effort not simply to accept traditional values (in the case of fishing that it is right to fish the way you do). Reference to tradition and the way things have always been done is not necessarily a good idea because it could be a choice of convenience. On the other hand, there is no point in rejecting traditional values just for the sake of rejecting them. The soul searching has to be thorough and not shy away from awkward questions. Thomas Aquinas defined conscience as

knowledge applied to an individual case[192]

and this is exactly what our Garonne man does when he decides that it's okay to fish the way he does. The same applies should he decide that it is not okay. There is nothing mysterious about the soul-searching exercise and the subsequent decision based on conscience – the word is of Latin origin and literally means "with knowledge". Conscience, whether philosophers like it or not, does shape moral decisions. Everybody has a conscience and everybody uses it. It is just as well because conscience is among many other things an internal check against choices too personally tainted and a safeguard against pure logic running wild. With all its soul-searching, the concept of conscience is a bit like the anti-virus software you have installed on your computer: it should alert you when it spots something fishy.

To act on the basis of knowledge seems reasonable enough although some philosophers would hotly dispute this, questioning such knowledge in the first place. On the practical side of things, decisions have to be made on some basis, and positive knowledge in the sense of science or scientific facts has the advantage of being ascertainable regardless of creed. Gravity is knowledge that can be shared by everybody, whereas an experience like tree hugging is of limited accessibility. You can imagine what it is like but that is not quite the same as knowing. Like many things in philosophy "application of knowledge to activity" sounds seductively simple, but beware! Apparent simplicity in philosophy doesn't always easily translate into real life. Just as

192 http://plato.stanford.edu/entries/conscience-medieval/

177

in fishing. The other day I was going to visit friends in Swindon whom I hadn't seen for quite some time. I decided to combine pleasure with pleasure and packed my fishing gear. I hadn't been reservoir or quarry fishing for ages, spending all my available fishing time in Scotland or Ireland. So on day two of my visit I suggested that we should have a little dinner party the following day. I would catch and cook the trout. Great idea – and preparations started right away, inviting people and shopping.

I had made enquiries as to where I was going to fish beforehand so all I had to do now was ring the fishery and book. "Yes, I would like the boat," I confirmed when asked. And "Yes, no problem," the fishery manager said I could take a few trout more if I paid for them. I was in no hurry the next morning. After all this was a put-and-take fishery. I inwardly concurred with all the Scottish and Irish prejudice that English reservoir fishing really isn't cricket. Anyway, I set off for about an hour's drive and arrived at the fishery at midday. Before starting to fish I glanced at the fishing log and noticed that most fish the day before were caught with a Montana nymph. Slightly disdainful I thought that the fly wouldn't matter anyway because these were tame, dumb rainbows I was going to catch. Nothing like the clever Scottish or Irish brownies. Anything really would do the trick. I tried everything in my box and everything failed and I didn't ask any of my fellow anglers for a Montana. They all caught fish – from the bank. I sat in the only available boat (presumably reserved for fools like me) in the middle of a pond watching beautiful rainbows being caught left, right and centre. And surely one or two of my fellow anglers must have wondered about that guy in the boat trying so hard and getting nowhere. The Montana was the common knowledge of the local fishermen that was meant to be shared. It was offered to me on a silver plate in that fishing log and I foolishly chose to ignore it. A case of prejudice and pride – the latter I had to swallow when among roars of laughter I ordered a fish curry in the Indian restaurant where the dinner party finally took place.

Aesthetics

Aesthetics is at first glance beautiful, boundless subjectivity. If something strikes you as beautiful – a sight, an experience, anything pleasantly sensual – you naturally tend to approve of it. Aesthetics is a contributory factor in moral approval or disapproval. It is part really of your moral values and beyond what you think or know the world is like. If a group of people share certain values and conventions they will also share to a significant degree what they think of as beautiful or ugly. Robbery, for example, is wrong and correspondingly the scene of people held at gunpoint is particularily ugly. There is a coherence in everybody's perception and interpretation of the world which shows in aesthetic attitudes.

Evolutionary theory explains beauty by its function to attract for the purpose of reproduction. Function, it is said, also determines, for example, our relation to flowers:

Humans as do many animals and insects, have an innate capacity to find flowers beautiful. This seems to have evolved in us in response to one of the evolved functions of flowers which is to provide information about the plant. Our appreciation of the beauty of flowers may well be innate or instinctive and be an adaptive response to colourful cues in the environment which originally helped primitive hominid species to find sources of food. With experience flowers tell us a lot about the ripeness of a plant's fruit.[193]

I was pleased to find this: bringing home trout instead of flowers just shows that I have left the primitive stage way behind me. Angling is a higher form of living, after all! But seriously, this leads back to the discussion about determinism, the view that whatever you do or are is determined by some evolutionary or biological fact. There is, presumably, more to life than evolution as there is more to beauty than the survival of the prettiest. A good way to open the mind for questions of beauty beyond the obvious is the following Shakespearean sonnet:

193 http://www.beautyworlds.com/orchids.htm This is a very interesting site – don't be deceived by the design.

O how much more doth beauty beauteous seem
By that sweet ornament which truth doth give!
The rose looks fair, but fairer we it deem
For that sweet odour which doth in it live.
The canker-blooms have full as deep a dye
As the perfum'd tincture of the roses,
Hang on such thorns, and play as wantonly
When summer's breath their mask'd buds discloses:
But for their virtue only is their show
They live unwoo'd and unrespected fade,
Die to themselves. Sweet roses do not so;
Of their sweet deaths are sweetest odours made.
And so of you, beauteous and lovely youth,
When that shall vade, by verse distills your truth.[194]

The idea that beauty is linked to ethics, is, as you rightly surmised, nothing new in the world of philosophy. The Greeks called the idea *kalokagathia*, that is the union of beauty, truth and goodness. In the 18th century the Earl of Shaftesbury revived the idea and inspired among others his Scottish philosopher colleague Frances Hutcheson to write a treatise the title of which is a neat summary of the concept: "An Inquiry into the Original of our Ideas of Beauty and Virtue; in two Treatises – I. Concerning Beauty, Order, Harmony, Design – II. Concerning Moral Good and Evil." [195]

We are under permanent siege by beautiful and happy people. The need for beauty is, however, real and not a mere fancy of the advertising industry. Just think how you try to embellish your work environment, for example, by hanging a beautiful picture on the wall. Or by placing a beautiful object on your desk – on mine there is the fly with which I caught a 25-pound trevally. In order to fully appreciate the importance of beauty and its link to ethics, think of statements such as "life is good" or "it's wrong to steal". Then replace the moral for the aesthetic words, e.g. "life is beautiful", "it is not beautiful to steal" and you'll often find the words express the same notions. I think this would go uncontested up to the moment when it comes to the crunch, that is, defining right and wrong, good and bad. This lands us inevitably back in basic positions and values such as animal rights and environmentalism. The point here is not to chew the cud but to draw attention to the power of the

194 *The Complete Works of William Shakespeare*, Spring Books, London (1976), p.1049.
195 This is the title of the second edition in 1726. Shaftesbury's ideas also influenced Berkeley, Butler and Hume.

aesthetic side of all the issues involved.

The language of beauty is often more plausible than the language of reason. This is why beauty – notions of beauty – are of such eminent importance in ethics and communication.

Some values can and do change. This seems the natural course of things. Consider the setting of a lake or a river you find strikingly beautiful or a particular spot which gives you great aesthetic pleasure – what is it that makes such a place beautiful for you? What is it that makes people agree that this or that is a beautiful view and why is it that, for example, some people are thrilled by pictures of icebergscapes and others feel a cold shiver looking at them? What are the values and conventions – is there beauty out there in the first place?

Landscape is one of the central aesthetic pleasures of fishing; thinking about it is equally pleasurable if it's done as in Malcolm Andrews' Landscape and Western Art. The first paragraph is a fanfare which promises some fascinating exploration – and this is one of the books which gives you much more than it promises. Anyway, here's that first paragraph – just give it a thought next time you admire the scenery around you:

A 'landscape', cultivated or wild, is already artifice before it has become the subject of a work of art. Even when we simply look we are already shaping and interpreting. A landscape may never achieve representation in a painting or photograph; none the less, something significant has happened when land can be perceived as 'landscape'. We may well follow an impulse to sketch or photograph a particular tract of land in view and call the resulting picture a 'landscape'. Whether or not we are artists, we have been making this kind of mental conversion for centuries. The habit is part of the whole history of our relationship with the physical environment, and the visual tradition of landscape representation from the start has been one vital element in that relationship. [195]

Among the many exciting lines of enquiry this opens, the one implied by:

Even when we simply look we are already shaping and interpreting [196]

---

196 Malcolm Andrews, *Landscape and Western Art*, Oxford University Press, New York (1999), p.1.

is in the present context the most pertinent. Have a look now at the picture painted by the following words:

Fish also show signs of distress when they are taken out of the water and allowed to flap around in a net or on dry land until they die. Surely it is only because fish do not yelp or whimper in a way that we can hear that otherwise decent people can think it a pleasant way of spending an afternoon to sit by the water dangling a hook while previously caught fish die slowly beside them.[197]

The angler sits in a scene of great natural beauty and everything emits harmony. By brushing in the slowly dying fish, Singer wins an excellent point because the appeal of aesthetics goes straight to the heart. Consider now an alternative description of basically the same situation. A probably otherwise decent person, Henry David Thoreau, writes of the pickerel of Walden pond:

Ah, the pickerel of Walden! When I see them lying on the ice, or in the well which the fisherman cuts in the ice, making a little hole to admit the water, I am always surprised by their rare beauty, as if they were fabulous fishes, they are so foreign to the streets, even to the woods, foreign as Arabia to our Concord life. They possess a quite dazzling and transcendent beauty which separates them by a wide interval from the cadaverous cod and haddock whose fame is trumpeted in our streets. They are not green like the pines, nor gray like the stones, nor blue like the sky; but they have, to my eyes, if possible, yet rarer colors, like flowers and precious stones, as if they were the pearls, animalized nuclei or crystals of Walden water. They, of course, are Walden all over and all through; are themselves small Waldens in the animal kingdom, Waldenses.[198]

Here the fish are right in the centre of the picture and very few readers will automatically in their mind's eye see cruelty and all that. There is nothing disturbing in Thoreau's picture, there is nothing wrong. The force of aesthetics is considerable and aesthetics involves the very same questions as morals. Enquiries into what is beautiful and what is good take place in different factual contexts but are bound to grapple with the same questions.

---

197 Peter Singer, *Animal Liberation*, Avon Books, New York (1991), p.172.
198 Henry David Thoreau, *Walden and Other Writings*, Metro Books, New York (2001), p.236. In this passage Thoreau the fisherman speaks. There is also Thoreau the vegetarian. See http://www.ivu.org/history/usa19/thoreau.html

One facet of conscience is its function as a sort of anti-virus software. Concomitant to this, your sense of aesthetics comes into the deliberating process in fishing matters. An oil-soaked bird is just as much an insult to the aesthetic sense as is a bird tangled up in discarded line. The point is that beside all the scrutinising, evaluating, rationalising, listening to inner voices or feeling little nudges of moral sentiment there is also an aesthetic side to ethics. A great number of things are decided on visual arguments. These might be very deceptive now and then but they figure in moral deliberations all the same. After all we have said about facts, conscience and aesthetics, what do you make of the following?

Mullet Snatching

For Sam Baker

The pick-up clattered out of sunset, shaken
To the Phillips screws by the washboard
Dirt road. We crossed inland waterways
To the highway and the bridge over
The Banana River in better time
Than time should allow.

Sam was master
Of our fish-as-catch-can expedition; my father
And I knew nothing of mullet except that
They were vegetarians and wouldn't fall
For any sort of bait, and couldn't be
Seined – legally, that is.

On the bridge in the closing folds
Of darkness, Sam lowered the Coleman
Lantern over the side till it hovered
A yard above the surface – a spinning
Plumb-bob twisting kinks out of the rope.
A stain of light spread across the water
And sank a few feet down. We could see
The surface sliding under the light, but
The water below held still, yellow-green
And hazy, like sunlit air swimming with dust.

Sam swang his bamboo pole out over
The river, the hook – a treble big
As an anchor – swinging on the steel
Line like a pendulum slowing. And when
It had swung back, far under the bridge,
He let it drop. He held the pole –
Butt-end toward the sky – against
The side of the bridge. "Hold it
Steady, hard against the concrete,"
he said. "The fish can hear it scrape."

With our hooks planted on the sand
Floor of the river behind the pale
Bowl of light, we waited.
                    And into
The light-frozen patch of water,
The rangy mullet rose, circling, pulled in
To our lodestar.
            I wondered what
They were searching and hoping for.
Whatever it was, they didn't find it:
Sam would jerk up hard on his pole,
The line slicing through the current,
The hook swimming up from the bottom
Like a shark on scent of blood. As it
Tore through the swarm of fish, it might,
By chance, catch one in the belly
Or back; and Sam would heave him out,
Heavy and shaking crazy on his line.
When the school returned, filling
The space again where the bolt
Of lightning had struck, breaking
The light with the flash and flick
Of white bodies sleek as eels, I'd
Tug hard, and miss! – the hook flying
Loose and dancing into darkness.

My father and I tried again
And again, while Sam stacked up
The fish on the bridge like firewood.

I asked Sam how he did it, being too
Young not to; and he'd shrug and tell me
Luck, or words to that effect. I didn't
Believe him: It had to be a matter
Of timing, a trick, a skill. If I
Could zero on a moving target like
A duck hunter, or a quarterback ...
But Sam swore he pulled on a hunch,
And more often than not, he'd get one,
Snagged through the eye, snatched
Clean through the tail.
                    We quit
At a baker's dozen – eleven for Sam
And two for my father. As luck,
Or whatever the word is, would
Have it, I had only a wet hook
Yanked from light and brackish
Water time and again.
                    I was
Too old, perhaps, to trust what
I didn't know. Without realizing,
I had already lost more than I knew I had to lose.[199]

What a story Malcolm Glass, the author, tells us here! What a scene, what a gripping poem – the loneliness, that bridge, that lamp just over the water, the three people bent over the parapet looking down. Then the fish being pulled up sending silver-glittery rays into the darkness, the mullet piling up, on the bridge. The graphic detail about the eyes, the tail, the belly together with that "I wonder what they were searching and hoping for" are really masterful: there is something eerie about this. The hooks dancing aimlessly in the dark before they're buried again in the sand – frightening imagery. There is no mention of piscatorial achievement, nor pride, nor is there any pleasure or that feeling of camaraderie born out of successful common experience. Also very strange: "and two for my father" – not "two for us". I wonder about the father-son relationship there. It's a sad, gloomy picture.[200]

---

199 *Wetting our Lines Together*, Editors Allen Hoey, Cynthia Hoey, Daniel J. Moriarty, An Anthology of Recent North American Fishing Poems, Tamarack Editions, Syracuse, New York, pp.55–57.
200 I have never tried myself for mullet. Apparently it is possible to catch them with the fly. See Paul Morgan, *Saltwater Flyfishing*, Coch-y-Bonddu Books, Machynlleth, Wales (1998), Chapter IV.

This is not the sort of picture you would like Ellen to see (remember Ellen and Bambi?). Gerald L. Smith, in that superb article of his "Eating Bambi: Disney Comes to Dixie", addresses among other abuses one he calls "slob-hunting" and explains why:

> *I speak of these things to my hunter safety students, reminding them that hunters must be careful of their public image if we want to protect the future of hunting and have support for hunting as they grow up. I speak of deer hunting and the practise of displaying deer across the hoods of jeeps and trucks. I note that this spoils meat but it also spoils the hunter's image. I tell the story of the pair of deer hunters I saw in a nearby town who drove back and forth on the main street honking and waving, making sure everyone saw them with the deer on the hood of their jeep. They had no idea of the offense they created. Although they lived in an area where the deer herd was large and hunting was common, they had no notion of the large number of non hunters who now live all through our county and who are passionate to ban deer hunting. These thoughtless hunters had given their opponents yet another illustration to use against hunters.[201]*

Like the mullet-snatching scene, the deer display picture is aesthetically extremely unsatisfying – the sense of beauty is not satisfied. Keepnets are an issue when, for example, whitefish which at the end of the day are going to be killed, are in the highest summer temperatures kept in tiny keepnets. There they suffocate due to lack of oxygen and can be seen by the people passing by on the sailing boats and other pleasure craft. They are an "illustration" against fishing. This is not the aesthetics that advertises for angling. And there is another point in this: the dying or dead whitefish are, like the deer on the bonnet, getting too much heat. As a result the firm and tasty whitefish meat will be pulpy and a culinary non-event. Waste. The proper way is to kill the whitefish immediately after the catch, clean it and put it into an icebox. That way it will be a delicacy. Fishing for whitefish in the right manner is an aesthetically satisfying experience all the way through to the dinner table. And should you have guests at home, a glorious meal of whitefish filets is the best possible advertisement for angling.

Aesthetics isn't just visual. Imagine a picture-postcard early morning on a little loch in the Scottish Highlands. No wind. There's thick mist hanging

201 http://smith2.sewanee.edu/gsmith/Texts/Hunting/EatingBambi.html

just over the water waiting to be chased away by the sun and the wind. There are two boats and this morning I am the first one out. There isn't too much litter in the boat and no bailing out to do – so, off I go. The mist is so thick that I can hardly see my hands on the oars, yet my head is clear of the low mist.

To an onlooker on that day, a strange sight that must have been, my head gliding above the mist. Anyway, sun and wind did their job and I settled expectantly for the first drift. The scenery, the quiet, gentle tapping of the waves against the boat – what a morning, what a glorious day in the making! That is, until I was rudely awakened by a high-pitched engine noise. One of those two-stroke four-horsepower nervous little dentist drill stinkers. To my utter amazement (I have fished that loch for years and never ever was there a boat with an outboard) I saw in the distance the second boat speeding uplake. I sat there temporarily paralysed – a trout could have taken my fly three times over and I wouldn't have reacted. The guys in the other boat seemed to be enjoying themselves: to correct the drift even for just a few metres they would use the engine. They regularly cut their drifts halfway and moved busily about that lochan as if to give it a thoroughly good mixing. Why not use an electric engine? In a situation like that, a conventional engine is aesthetically a bad idea and it is bad advertising for angling – just think of the walkers, bird watchers and inspiration-hungry romantic poets passing by.

Before long my fellow anglers got close enough for me to have a chance to look at them. They sported assault outfits which would have been the pride of any military fashion show – all that was missing was the black shoe shine on their faces – the assault make-up. Anyway their whole attitude to fishing seemed rooted in the idea that to catch a trout is something akin to storming a terrorist stronghold. They most certainly weren't soldiers, because the fishing soldiers I have met so far have a sound sense of aesthetics. Apart from that, why should they be wearing their working outfits when fishing? Anyway, the two crack trout-troopers went about their business and I went about mine. But I followed them all day out of the corner of my eye – for some reason a sort of competitive spirit had taken hold of me. I am happy to report that at the end of the day I clearly caught more than the two of them together and I couldn't help thinking: serves you right, you noisy … After all, there is justice in the world…

The black shoe shine is worth a second look because there is something quintessential about it. Imagine my two friends with the noise generator actually hitting on the idea of painting their faces black. I don't know, but I

187

almost bet that, if the noise hadn't hammered all the sense out of them, they would have started feeling a bit ridiculous – incongruent. Their sense of aesthetics would have revolted, they would have felt that something about painting their faces black was not right.

Aesthetics and ethics in angling are closely related. This, however, does not mean accepting everything at face value – that's rarely a good idea in philosophy or in real life. Aesthetics doesn't stand for an uncritical attitude – the sense of beauty wants to be informed and listened to, so to speak. Here is an example of what this can mean. The scene of the action was a lough in the west of Ireland. Fishing was at the time limited to a few private and public boats. I considered myself very lucky to get on without prior booking a couple of months ahead, thanks to another angler who had cancelled his reservation. The unknown fellow angler was probably a salmon expert – the weather forecast predicted a scorcher. Anyway, arrangements were made over the telephone the day before; the boat would be ready for me at nine. The manager regretted that he would be unable to meet me because of some other business. So he informed me of some shallows and ropes that hold a fish cage in one of the bays and told me that I would find a precise map in the shelter for anglers. Okay.

Keen as mustard I woke up very, very early and after a hearty breakfast headed for the lough. There was no traffic and I found the place in no time at all. It was quarter to eight and to my surprise the boat was ready waiting for me there. A beautiful boat with a swivel chair – what luxury! I was very pleased and really eager so after picking up the map in the rest room I decided to mount the rods on the lough somewhere – it was all calm. I wanted to be out there fast. The engine started first time and off I went. As I headed out I studied the map. No problem, everything fine. I accelerated. Too much for my hat. It sailed into the lough and landed so awkwardly that it sank immediately. It was a present from one of my apprentices supposed to bring me luck. It didn't curb my blind enthusiasm.

Off I went again. I accelerated. Full steam this time. Seconds later there was an almighty scratching noise and then a bump. I was thrown forward and when I picked myself cursingly up, switched off the engine and looked around, I saw that I was hung up on the shallows. Firmly. No damage to the boat nor the engine – phew! There was only one thing to do: out I went and pushed the boat back and hopped in again. The water was, as you would expect, just exactly above welly height. I recovered and continued, only to hit two more shallows and one of the ropes until I realised that I had been holding the map upside down. But it didn't end there. There wasn't going to be any plain sailing that day.

For once the weather forecast was right: it was a scorcher in Western Ireland! In order not to get heat stroke (it was that hot!) I made an impromptu hat with my handkerchief which I soaked in water before putting onto my head. Lovely – very refreshing, the water trickling down over my face. I repeated the soaking when the hanky dried up. I fished doggedly but no fish came my way. The heat was going from bad to worse and the light was so glaring that my eyes, despite sun glasses, started to hurt: a burning sensation which got worse and worse as time went by so that my eyes started to water. It really hurt – and for the first time that day, it stopped me and I switched on my brain. True, the light was glaring and it was hot but that couldn't be the reason for my watering eyes. Tears were pouring down. What was it then? The reason was really staring at me. That lough was tidal! So I washed my eyes with the mineral water I had with me.

Minutes later I saw for the first time that day the things around me. The splendid scenery, the glorious light and the inside of the boat with wellies, drying socks, the rod tubes, wax jacket, the rod sleeves (which normally stay with the tubes in the car) – it was a mess really – struck me as incongruent, an aesthetic insult reflecting my whole attitude that day. All that can be said in my honour is that I decided there and then to pack up. I chugged back past the rope and the shallows by now inwardly smiling at my foolishness earlier. I landed the boat with a perfect manoeuvre. There was man at the jetty to help me tie the boat up: the manager. He was furious and he said and looked so. I was flabbergasted until I understood what had happened: I had been that hour and a quarter early and I simply assumed that the boat at the jetty was meant for me. It wasn't. I had inadvertently taken another angler's boat! At the precise moment when I took his boat he was in the main building with the manager; when they came out, they saw only the wake of "my" boat in the distance. My fellow angler was apparently so upset by this and probably by the weather as well that he lost all interest and went back home. Highly embarrassing.

These occurrences weren't simply mishaps. My actions were guided by a sort of blind, greedy eagerness which prevented me from "listening" to knowledge (facts), reason and beauty. Take, for instance, the two rod tubes. Experience, reason and beauty would normally have told me in unison that

189

it was an altogether bad idea. Those tubes are made of aluminium and tend to roll about in the boat, producing a really unpleasant clanking noise. A practical and aesthetic annoyance of the first order. The same applies to going at full speed. Everything would have made me normally opt for going very slowly. I could have watched what was going on around me, maybe even spotted some fish, and I would have had the pleasure of a beautiful morning presenting itself in all its glory. Beauty and reality cannot be separated just as beauty and morality are probably merely different sides of the same coin. Be that as it may, the most important message from this discussion of aesthetics is that if your approach and actual fishing satisfy your sense of beauty, it will very likely be excellent fishing. Bad or doubtful aesthetics doesn't make for good fishing.

There is certainly more to beauty than meets the eye. The entwinement of beauty and morality is clearly nothing new under the sun. However, aesthetics isn't discussed in *The Case for Animal Rights* nor in *Animal Liberation*. The reason for this is that animal rights and animal liberation translated into reality mean radical change. What a "cruelty-free" society's aesthetics look like cannot be envisaged, just as in 1918 you couldn't predict really what the aesthetics of the Soviet Union were going to be. Advertising in the early Soviet Union was very colourful, cheerful and optimistic before it turned all grey.[202]

In the case of the "cruelty-free" society, however, one can make an educated guess about certain aspects because veganism has immediate practical consequences. A vegan does not eat or use animal products. No barbecues, no leather shoes. Grilled tofu and plastic sandals. Apart from that, try and imagine what cities and for that matter the countryside will look like with all animal life literally running wild. Or try and appreciate the cover design of vegan books and ask yourself if you would like elements of it as wallpaper. The point is that we can only guess the contours of what a "cruelty-free" society would look like – but we do know for certain that fishing would have no place there.

The extent to which aesthetics mirror basic values in philosophy and reality is shown in the case of a hooked sea trout leaping out of the water. Anti-anglers see this as torturing the creature, inflicting pain and suffering and violating the animal's rights and interests: in contrast, anglers see it as a

202 *Sowjetisches Reklamedesign der zwanziger Jahre,* edited by: Mikhail Anikst, Bangert Verlag, Munich.

moment of intense excitement that makes them just want to shout for joy – and back we are right in the middle of cruelty. The cheer is, of course, not jubilation at torture but an expression of the joy of the angler who has been taken by a fish. That leap, in the eyes of the angler, is pure beauty. This adds the final element to the discussion about cruelty. We have discussed the facts, we have discussed intention and now beauty and emotion. The conclusion is: fishing is factually, intentionally and aesthetically in no way cruel. And with that the chapter on cruelty is definitely closed.

Miss Bayle

Anglers don't see themselves as carbon-copy soldiers in the piscatorial army. They prefer to think of themselves as individualists. Yet if you look at angling catalogues it seems that industry and trade think they're all the same. Much angling advertising material seems to be churned out to the same formula. In one way or another the ideal hunting grounds are depicted or evoked and the other key visual is the object of desire, i.e. the fish still at large, or clasped trophy-like by the angler. These are the professional pictures.

The world's most silly category of photographs are fishing trophy amateur shots. Especially worth mentioning are those marvellous wide angle pictures showing three or more men holding a fish each. They could be, for example, holding fine two-pound brown trout. The wide-angle lens makes the scene even sillier than it is. The proportion of men to fish shrinks the latter into insignificance. The great majority of ordinary anglers in pictures like this sport a slightly barmy expression. They are not models used to posing. They're trying hard, extending their arms, holding the fish as close to the camera as possible. Good thinking, but the impression usually is, given the anglers' facial expression, that they are holding their fish as far away from themselves as possible – as if the fish stank. On top of that the fish get the full benefit of the flashlight. The beautifully red speckled trout then become unidentifiable shiny objects. The red spots show only in the anglers' eyes. To an outsider, such photographs are meaningless, affording only fleeting interest and some amusement. They're like photographs of great stage productions. If you haven't been there, they're somehow lifeless.

To anglers, photographs of themselves with the fish caught are open books. There's the story of it all. There are also, in every instance of such amazing photographs, all the reasons why anglers go fishing – are compelled to fishing. There are as many sets of different reasons for going fishing as there are fishermen. But all the reasons are not an answer to the question why men fish.

Angling is somewhat like poetry, men are to be born so.[203]

There is little doubt that anglers and poets have a lot in common. Anglers and poets are often frowned on, for they are like as not at variance with the norm. While poets have no use for worms in the fridge, they tend also to be up and about when everybody is fast asleep. Or take the weather. While everybody yearns for sunshine, the angler dreams of a slightly overcast sky, a gentle breeze and scattered showers. Sometimes anglers want lots of rain and so do some poets too, for then that inspired productive melancholy gets hold of them. Anglers, like poets, have to be good observers and their analytical powers must be well developed. They certainly share an interest in discovery, harmony and beauty – even urban anglers and poets do. While it is true that both are often eyed with suspicion, their achievements are usually greeted with approval and enthusiasm. There is nothing like a big fish or a beautiful poem to convince the sceptics. So it's easy to see that angling and poetry have a lot of common ground, but what makes anglers and poets tick is far from obvious. "Men are to be born so" is not a satisfactory explanation because a fishing-gene-statement like it doesn't really tell us much. Why do fishermen fish and poets write poetry? I sometimes feel there is an answer hiding in this poem by Petrarch:

A pure white hind appeared to me
With two gold horns, on green grass,
Between two streams, in a laurel's shade,
At sunrise, in the unripe season.

Her aspect was so sweet and proud
I left all my labour to follow her:
As a miser, in search of treasure,
Makes his toil lose its bitterness in delight.

'Touch me not,' in diamonds and topaz,
was written round about her lovely neck:
'it pleased my Lord to set me free.'

The sun had already mounted to mid-day
My eyes were tired with gazing, but not sated,

203 Izaak Walton, *The Compleat Angler*, Introduction by Thomas McGuane, Ecco Press, New Jersey (1995), p.39.

When I fell into the water, and she vanished.[204]

Splash, there goes the answer. Around 1330 Petrarch was spending a whole summer in a village called Lombez in the South West of France, about 40–50 minutes' drive of Toulouse. Driving there from that direction you pass the bridge over the river Save into the village. Lombez is a beautiful little village of the type where dogs still take a nap on the main road. The main attraction of the village is the Sainte Marie cathedral, the beginnings of which date back to the 6th century AD. To call it an attraction would do it an injustice – it's a magnificent landmark. There is a simple, breathtaking Gothic grandeur about it. It's a work of art of engulfing beauty and you can literally sense the awe-inspiring force emanating from it. The stained glass draws beautiful, ever-changing colour patterns on the mighty pillars which branch out at the top like palm trees. If you like that kind of experience the Sainte Marie cathedral definitely *mérite un détour*.

Should you be interested in *pétanque*, a Mediterranean game of bowls, you'll find Lombez even more attractive. *Pétanque* is played outdoors in public places all over France, but especially in the South. Ideally on gritty gravely, sandy ground. It is played with rather heavy metal balls, called boules. The idea is to place your boules as closely as possible to the cochonette, a little target ball. The nearest boule to the target wins. Sounds easy and looks easy when you see the champs at work. It's like fly casting. If a master of the art places his fly on a beermat thirty yards away you think it's dead easy. That is, up to the moment when the rod is handed to you.

Anyway, weather permitting the locals of Lombez gather every day around the town hall for their game. The town hall is on the right hand side just after bridge over the Save. Half of the *pétanque* arena is along the banks of the Save, which flows a few metres down from playing level. There is a little wall to sit on and to prevent boules rolling down the bank into the river. On the other side of the road facing the entrance of the town hall, there is an estate agent – the billboards glaring in yellow and black. Really a bit out of place in such historical surroundings. Just past the town hall are the traffic lights. Straight on it's the main road through Lombez and to the right runs the Samatan road. The ground around the town hall is ideal for *pétanque* and so are the plane trees which are the most perfect parasols. To play in the

---

204 "Una candida cerva sopra l'herba", translated by Tony Kline. See www.tkline.freeserve.co.uk

gloriously rich and mild summer nights the *pétanque* players have installed lighting in the trees.

The Save flows lazily through picturesque villages and is a water with mainly carp, roach, perch and pike. One recent afternoon I sat on that wall above the Save idly watching the water, the *pétanque* matches and the scenery alternatingly. A troop of schoolchildren made their way across the bridge to the sports ground on the other side. Merry voices and laughter marked their progress. Two flics set up shop on the road to Samatan. They parked their car a little off the road, then stood nearby. With easy movement of the wrist and a well-studied pose (maybe they learn it at the police academy there) one officer circled his police whistle so it looked like a propeller in motion. A cyclist with a baguette under one arm took a short cut across the *pétanque* grounds to avoid the traffic lights. He zigzagged between the players and the boules, stopping twice to have a little chat. He turned onto the Samatan road exactly in front of the police officers. An exchange of greeting nods. As the cyclist disappeared out of view, a fisherman entered the scene. Interesting.

The police officers thought so too, because they involved the piscator in a conversation. The fisherman leaned his rod against a tree in order to show the officers something in his fishing bag. Comprehending and appreciative nods from the forces of the law. Further lively discussion. After a while the fisherman made his way past the *pétanque* players with the same routine as the cyclist. He was obviously well known: "Hello Pierre" here, "Hello Pierre" there. And there was, of course, a full volley of good-humoured jests and banter. The usual stuff every fisherman knows: the address of the nearest fishmonger, taking worms for a swim, catching more of a cold than anything else and so on. Pierre also must have heard them for the umpteenth time and made his way unperturbed over the bridge and then to the left, taking the path along the bank. He obviously intended to fish further downstream. After I had lost sight of him, I turned to the *pétanque* again and chewed over that question of why men fish.

Here right in front of me I had a superb antithesis to fishing: *pétanque*. What a great idea. Apart from its suitability for all ages and levels of skill, it's a great socialiser. Everybody can and does play – it's a classless recreational activity. The equipment in comparison to fishing is simple and cheap and, at least in the South, *pétanque* is a year-round pursuit. No tickets required either. Why do the Pierres of this world prefer the solitude of the riverbank to the good, jovial company of the *pétanque* arena?

A wolf-whistle which could only have been directed at a girl woke me from my musings. And indeed towards the bridge walked who I later learned to be Mademoiselle Laura Bayle, the manageress of the estate agents. The shapely Miss Bayle was the cause of many near-accidents on the main road through Lombez. As a teenager she had once tried in vain to participate in a beauty contest. The jury flatly refused to let her compete on the grounds that with her in the contest the result would be a foregone conclusion. Not to worry, Miss Bayle apparently had other ideas about life than a career as a glamour model. As my eyes followed her passing the bridge, something abruptly stopped her in her stiletto tracks. She froze in a position not unlike that of Jim's when he spotted those cows in the distance. As she shouted, "Hold on to it, Pierre!" all eyes turned first to her and then in the downstream direction. There, everybody now saw Pierre leaning backwards, heels dug in, rod arched and holding it with obvious effort. He was into a leviathan. Pierre had come upstream again and had chosen a spot opposite the downstream end of the *pétanque* grounds. Along with everybody else I watched, mouth agape.

A young *pétanque* player recovered his senses first and sprinted past Miss Bayle without even a hint of a sideward glance. There might have been a fishing gene hiding somewhere in that young man. In no time he was beside Pierre, who obviously knew his business. He instructed his assistant to open the net, extend the telescopic arm and then to put the net into the water so that it really lay on the ground not visible to the fish. Then the assistant crouched to give as little silhouette as possible. So did Pierre a short while later. In the meantime quite a few passers-by had stopped at the bridge, because if it was worth Miss Bayle's time to look at something, it must be worth theirs, too. Only minutes later the schoolchildren came back from the sport ground and joined the onlookers.

Pétanque was abandoned. Everybody, including the two police officers, stood or sat on the little wall following the events and commenting. The crowd grew. Some people even stood behind Pierre. The flics jumped into action. They whistled the encroaching onlookers back and then went onto the other side to effectively cordon off the area. It wasn't a fight really – no runs, no splashing. It was a tug of war and a short one at that, as is often the case with really big pike. After about twenty minutes a pike of 37 pounds was landed amidst great cheers and applause.

197

In the crowd watching the great catch was also René, the landlord and chef of the Restaurant des Pyrénées. "Is there going to be a party tonight, Pierre?" he shouted across the Save. "You bet, and everybody is welcome!" came the answer immediately. "Bring it along then now!" René commanded. Pierre's strong arms went under the fish and lifted it. Then he started walking towards the crowd, which drew back respectfully and full of admiration. The two police officers went a few steps ahead of Pierre, and behind him came the assistant with rod and net. Again spontaneous applause. The procession passed Miss Bayle, and Pierre on impulse winked and was granted a smile out of this world – angelic. A lesser man would have fainted. In the five minutes it took the procession to reach the Restaurant des Pyrénées, René had covered a table on the terrace with greenery. There the pike was laid out to be marvelled at by all.

A few hours later the party was in full swing under the plane trees. Tables and chairs had been provided by the restaurant and the town hall. With everybody assisting and contributing this, that or the other. The tables were laden with local goodies and everybody indulged with enthusiasm in the regional wines. The main attraction, greatly acclaimed as the very best of all times were, of course, the pike quenelles. It was a sumptuous, bucolic feast of great beauty. Happy faces all round. The accordion played and as Pierre and Miss Bayle opened the dance, it was suddenly plain for all to see that if there was ever a perfect match this was it. If you listened you could already hear the wedding bells ringing. This pike would be talked about for generations to come. I raised my glass in celebration as did the Lombezians, and this took its toll. I was feeling distinctly tired. Seconds before I dozed off, I thought that I understood why men go fishing, but I was too tired to get a hold on the answer. Like a trout coming short, wisdom disappeared with a swirl heading for God only knows where. Wisdom might have eluded me, but about one thing I was then and now in no doubt: there is nothing wrong with fishing. Fishing is good. Life is beautiful.

APPENDIX

The Essential Bibliography

For the full bibliography, updates, additional source materials and comments please visit

www.philosofish.ch

where you can also contact me.

The following three books touch upon many of the issues discussed in *Hook, Line and Thinker*:

Fishing and Thinking, A.A. Luce, Swan Hill Press, Shrewsbury, England (1990). ISBN 1 85310 151 6
Animal Liberation, Peter Singer, Avon Books, New York (1990). ISBN 0-380-71333-0
The Case for Animal Rights, Tom Regan, University of California Press, Berkeley and Los Angeles, USA (1983). ISBN 0-520-05460-1 (pbk)

Key Words

A

Aesthetics

Study and analysis of the beautiful in art or nature. There are two fundamentally different approaches to aesthetics. One school of thought supposes that there are no objective values; that beauty is in the eye of the beholder. Other thinkers claim that there are objective values. Parallel positions are held in ethics.

Animal

For the discussion of animal rights an animal is a living creature which is not a human being or a plant. The biological definition: present day classification of life based on genetic sequencing places animals and human beings in a large group called eukaryotes. Eukaryotes are all living organisms with one or more cells featuring nuclei and organelles. Eukaryotes cover the kingdom of animals, fungi, plants and protists. Animals are distinguished from the plant kingdom by being heterotrophic: nutrients are obtained by digestion of plant or animal matter. Plants in contrast obtain nutrients by chemical processes such as photosynthesis. Prokaryotes, the other large group include organisms which lack nucleus and organelles – bacteria belong to this group. Note: this classification is bound to change at some future time.

Anthropocentrism

Anthropocentrism looks at the world from a human point of view and places man at the centre of things. Theistic anthropocentrism holds that man is at the centre of God's creation, while atheistic anthropocentrism understands man to be at the the centre of a purely material universe.

Anthropomorphism

Anthropomorphism is the attribution of human characteristics to non-human entities like trees and animals.

Aquinas

St. Thomas Aquinas (1225–1274 AD) is undoubtedly the greatest figure in medieval philosophy and one of the most important philosophers ever. His great achievment was to combine Aristotelian teaching with Christian philosophy. In the 19th century his work was declared by the Catholic Church as the basis of Christian philosophy. For animal rights philosophers St. Thomas Aquinas and Aristotle are the proverbial red rag.

Aristotle

Like St. Thomas Aquinas, Aristotle (384–324 BC) is a towering figure in the history of philosophy. He was the tutor of Alexander the Great and a scholar of breathtaking universality. He founded zoology and was, of course, also interested in fish. His description of a species of catfish was derided right into the 19th century when a Swiss scholar, Louis Agassiz, discovered that the Aristotelian description matched the fish he observed in some American rivers. Since 1906 this catfish has been officially called *silurus aristotelis*.

Autonomy

In order to be a moral agent a person must be autonomous, that is, free to deliberate his actions. If a person is not autonomous, his decisions are determined by physical forces rather than controlled by his free will.

B

Biology

Biology is the science of living things and divides into two major groups: zoology and botany. Zoology is the study of animals and botany the study of plant life. These are in turn split up into many subdivisions.

Bioethics

Bioethics is the specialised study of ethics in modern medical research and treatment.

C

Christianity

Christianity is the religion based on the life and teachings of Jesus Christ. Christianity today is the principal religion in Europe and the Americas. There are nominally many Christian churches but common to them, in ethical terms, are the Ten Commandments. These are by and large still the basis of most people's daily ethical life, for the simple reason that they are in principle as valid now as when they were given by Moses. Christianity even for those who don't practice religion is the general cultural framework which provides the values we respect. What is called Western culture is based on Christianity.

Consequentialism

Consequentialism is a modern variant of utilitarianism. John Stuart Mill's definition of Utilitarianism is:

the creed which accepts as the foundation of morals, Utility, or the Greatest Happiness Principle, holds that actions are right in proportion as they tend to promote happiness, wrong as they tend to produce the reverse of happiness. By happiness is intended pleasure and the absence of pain; by unhappiness, pain and the privation of pleasure.

Consequentialism holds that it is exclusively the outcome, the result of an action which decides between right and wrong. In the present context the most important version of consequentialism is Preference Utilitarianism. Actions are right insofar as they maximise people's preferences. Moral right is thus a function of people's preferences. There are no absolute rights or wrongs. In other words, the end justifies the means.

D

Darwin

Charles Darwin (1809–1882) is often held up as the most important scientist ever and his *The Origin of Species by Means of Natural Selection, or the Preservation of Favoured Races in the Struggle for Life* as the most important scientific book ever written. It has certainly been one of the most influential books of all time because it places the story of evolution and natural selection at the heart of all subsequent debate in biology, philosophy and religion.

Duty

A moral duty obliges you to act as morality prescribes. A legal duty obliges you to act in conformity to the law. Moral duties and legal duties are not necessarily identical. *See also* Right.

E

Empiricism

Empiricism holds that the source of all knowledge is experience. The mind at birth is a blank page – there are no innate ideas or knowledge.

Ethics

Ethics, or moral philosophy, is the systematic study and application of the ideas and concepts governing actions and attitudes in relation to right and wrong and good and bad.

Evolution

Evolution is the theory that all present life-forms, all present species, have developed from earlier forms of life. All life is said to have originated fromthe same primaeval soup, a biochemical mixture favourable to life. Along the evolutionary line, species appear and disapppear. Fossils are the record of change. Evolutionary change is brought about by natural selection. Natural selection is a process whereby those organisms best able to adapt to their given environment will reproduce best and thereby pass on their successful traits to future generations. Survival of the fittest.

F

Fascism

Fascism is the name for the totalitarian government of Benito Mussolini in Italy between 1922 and 1943. *See also* Totalitarian.

G

Gaia, Gaia hypothesis

Gaia is the name of the Greek earth goddess. The Gaia hypothesis is the theory according to which earth is a living being, a system aiming to attain an equilibrium by vast self-regulating mechanisms involving biochemical and physical processes. This means the earth controls its own environment.

Gene

A gene is the basic unit of heredity capable of transmitting traits to the next generation.

I

Ichthyology

Ichthyology is the scientific study of fish.

J

Jainism

Jainism is an ancient Indian religion. Its core is non-violence and compassion for all living beings. Jainists practise what they say to the letter. As they walk, they sweep the path in front of them so as not to crush a living being by stepping on it. Non-violence includes non-violence to plants. The Jainist diet is very restricted because plants are also living beings which must not be harmed.

L
Luce

A.A.Luce (1882–1977) fisherman and author of *Fishing and Thinking* was also the biographer and editor of the 18th century Irish philosopher George Berkeley.

M
Metaphysics

In the philosophical sense, metaphysics is the enquiry into the fundamental nature of reality.

N
Nazism

Nazism was the ideology of Adolf Hitler and the German National Socialist Party. Some key features of this ideology are a belief in the superiority of the Aryan race and a violent anti-Semitism. The latter led to the Holocaust. Hitler and the National Socialist Party ruled Germany between 1933 and 1945. *See also* Totalitarian.

R
Racism

Animosity and prejudice against people of other races. Belief in inherent superiority of a particular human race.

Rights

A legal right originates in the positive law, that is, the laws posited by the powers that be.

A moral right originates in the moral law, which is derived from morality itself.

Both types of rights always entail duties. Note: for consequentialists there are no moral rights although they frequently appeal to such rights.

P
Philosophy

The word originated in the Greek philos ("friend") and sophos ("wise"). Philosophy is the love of wisdom. It is the study of life and its meaning.

Primates

On the basis of evolutionary relationships zoologists classify the following mammal groups as primates: lemurs, lorises, tarsiers, monkeys, apes and human beings.

S

Sentient

According to animal rightists all sentient beings have rights.
The Oxford Modern English Dictionary (1992) defines "sentient" as follows:
Having the power of perception by the senses

The *Encarta-Dictionary* defines it as:
Conscious: capable of feeling and perception

Speciesism

The original definition in *Animal Liberation* is:
Speciesism is a bias in favour of the interests of members of one's own species and against those members of other species.
In the meantime, speciesism has found its way also into the *Encarta Dictionary* as:
Human assumption of superiority: the belief that the human race is superior to other species, and that exploitation of animals for the advantage of humans is justified.
Note how the dictionary definition amplifies the original statement in that it brings in the notions of race and exploitation. This is a fine illustration of how animal rights ideas creep in through the back door and also of the use of subtle political bias in supposedly impartial dictionaries.

Subjectivism

Subjectivist ethics simply means there are no objective moral values. Moral values are relative to individuals – what the individual feels or decides to be right or wrong is right or wrong. A variation of this theme is cultural relativism, which states that different cultures around the world have different values and that therefore there are no objective values.

T

Totalitarian

Dictatorial and centralised government by one party. Total control over all political, economic, social and cultural activities characterise totalitarian governments. Opposition or non-conformity are usually violently surpressed. Examples of totalitarian States are Germany under the Nazis and Italy under Benito Mussolini, the former Soviet Union and Cambodia under Pol Pot. Today, dictatorships such as Iraq and North Korea are examples of totalitarian States.

Animal Rights Quotes

"I believe in animal rights, human rights, land rights, water rights, air rights"
Rod Coronado, Twilight's Collection of Animal Rights Quotes / http://www.geocities.com/RainForest/Vines/2326/quote.html

"The life of an ant and that of my child should be granted equal consideration"
Michael W. Fox, Vice President, The Human Society of the United States, *The Inhumane Society*, New York, 1990

"We feel that animals have the same rights as retarded children"
Alex Pacheo, Director, PETA, New York Times, January 14, 1989

"We are not superior. There are no clear distinctions between us and animals"
Michael Fox, Washingtonian Magazine, February 1990

"What we must do is start viewing every cow, pig, chicken, monkey, rabbit, mouse, and pigeon as our family members"
Gary Yourofsky, ADAPTT (Animals Deserve Adequate Protection Today and Tomorrow); Quoted in "Activist devotes life to animal rights", Toledo Blade, June 24, 2001.

It's wrong to kill an animal for food but:
"In my view the secret killing of a normal happy infant by parents unwilling to be burdened with its upbringing would be no greater moral wrong than that done by parents who abstain from conceiving a child for the same reasons"
Peter Singer, *The New York Review of Books*, August 14, 1980
Source://http.//www.nybooks.com/articles/7324 /

When asked in a Q & A session which he would save, a dog, or a baby, if a boat capsized in the ocean:
"If it were a retarded baby and a bright dog, I'd save the dog"
Tom Regan, University of Wisconsin-Madison, October 27, 1989

"We have, then, no basic right against nature not to be harmed by those natural diseases we are heir to"
Tom Regan, *The Case for Animal Rights*

"If the death of one rat cured all diseases, it wouldn't make any difference to me"
Chris de Rose, Director, Last Chance for Animals

On the consequences of stopping animal research:
"Don't get the diseases in the first place, schmo"
(USA Today, July 27, 1994) Dan Mathews; PETA

"The optimum human population of earth is zero"
Dave Foreman, Earth First! Twilight's Collection
of Animal Rights Quotes

"We need a drastic decrease in human population if we ever hope to create a just and equitable world for animals"
Wicklund Freeman, Executive Director, Compassionate Action for Animals, No Compromise, September 1996

"Six million Jews died in concentration camps, but six billion broiler chickens will die this year in slaughterhouses"
Ingrid Newkirk, PETA, Washington Post, 1983

[The day should come when] *"all of the the forms of life... will stand before the court – the pileated woodpecker as well as the coyote and bear, the lemmings as well as the trout in the streams"*
William O. Douglas (late U.S. Supreme Court Justice), http://www.animal-rights.com/finally.html

"Religion has never befriended the cause of humaneness"
Henry Salt, 19th century animal rights pioneer

"Christianity is our foe. If animal rights is to succeed, we must destroy the Judeo-Christian religious tradition"
Peter Singer, *The Deweese Report*, November 1998

A short history of animal rights

600 BC–1789 AD: Vegetarianism
Evidence for vegetarianism goes as far back as the Greek poet Hesiod (c. 800 BC). The most prominent vegetarian of that early period was the mathematician Pythagoras. Throughout this period the reasons for being vegetarian were a compound of compassion, health and religious beliefs.

1789–1892: Animal Welfare
In 1789 the English Philosopher Jeremy Bentham introduced the idea that animals should be protected by law.
The day may come when the rest of the animal creation may acquire those rights which never could have been withheld from them but by the hand of tyranny. . . a full-grown horse or dog is beyond comparison a more rational, as well as a more conversable animal, than an infant of a day, or a week or even a month old. But suppose the case were otherwise, what would it avail? The question is not, can they reason? Nor can they talk? But, can they suffer? Why should the law refuse its protection to any sensitive being? The time will come when humanity will extend its mantle over everything which breathes...

From then on the pace accelerated:
1822 The House of Commons passes the Martin's Act, the world's first law for the protection of animals.
1824 The SPCA, the forerunner of the RSPCA, was founded. It was the world's first animal welfare society.
1847 Before this year the term vegetarianism was not known.
Vegetarianism before 1847 was called "the vegetable system of diet" or "the Pythagorean system". The word "vegetarianism" was coined at the constitutional meeting of The Vegetarian Society.
By the end of the 19th century Europe and the United States had animal welfare legislation, animal welfare societies and vegetarian societies. In 1908 the International Vegetarian Union which to this day unites the vegetarian societies of the world was founded.

1892–2003: Animal Rights
1892 *Animals' Rights* by Henry Salt is published and with it the history of animal rights proper begins.
1944 Foundation of the Vegan Society in England.
1970 Richard Ryder coins the term "speciesism".

1972 Ronnie Lee founds the Band of Mercy which in 1976 becomes the ALF (Animal Liberation Front)

1975 Peter Singer's *Animal Liberation* gives the animal rights movement a momentum which it has not lost since.

1977 The first International Congress for Animal Rights takes place at Trinity College Cambridge. A Declaration against speciesism is signed.

1980 PETA, People for the Ethical Treatment of Animals, is founded.

1983 Tom Regan's *The Case for Animal Rights* is published.

The last twenty years have witnessed an almost unchecked international proliferation of animal rights ideas. Many animal welfare societies and environmental organisations have drifted slowly but steadily from the concept of welfare to rights. Animal rights have also gained a foothold in the educational and political establishment. The threatened ban on hunting and the calls for the abolition of angling and most other fieldsports shows the confidence and power of the movement. Opposing ideas are having a bumpy ride presently but the tide might be turning.

For more background information, links and for an opportunity to comment and ask questions:

www.philosofish.ch

Index

Recommended reading from Merlin Unwin Books

THE FAR FROM COMPLEAT ANGLER
Tom Fort

Tom Fort, fishing correspondent for the *Financial Times*, travels to some exotic far-flung locations in search of trout, salmon, even dourado. He has fun with eels on the Test and takes his rods to Eastern   Europe and Brazil. This is a wonderful collection of fishing travels, interspersed with some profound thoughts about the sport of fishing and written by a man with a sharp eye for the absurd and the funny.

Hardback **£16.99**

Few can match his effortless essay style. This book levers fishing writing out of a rut – The Field

A HISTORY OF FLYFISHING
Conrad Voss Bark

With a delightful blend of wit and erudition Conrad Voss Bark tells the story of flyfishing, from the Macedonian 'plumes' of old to the hairwing streamers of today. He reviews the sport's formative protagonists: Juliana Berners, Robert Venables, Isaak Walton, Charles Cotton, Alfred Ronalds, George Kelson, Skues and Halford, Theodore Gordon, and many more.

Hardback **£25**
Paperback **£12.95**

An enchanting and learned book - The Field

CONFESSIONS OF A SHOOTING FISHING MAN
Laurence Catlow

Is it right to shoot and fish for pleasure? At the start of his sporting year, Laurence Catlow asks himself this central question. His sporting diary recording the high and lows of a sporting year in Cumbria often returns to this theme and in so doing tackles the controversial and highly topical issues in the fieldsports debate. Entertaining and disarmingly frank, Catlow presents powerful arguments in favour of shooting, fishing and hunting.

Hardback **£17.99**
Paperback **£9.99**

If you are looking for a present for a friend who shoots or fishes, then you need look no further than this book
– Roger Scruton, The Times

All these books are available by direct mail, next-day despatch, from
Merlin Unwin Books
7 Corve Street
Ludlow
Shropshire
SY8 1DB
UK.

Credit card orders on:
Tel (00 44) 1584 877456
Fax (00 44) 1584 877457

Or you can buy books via our website
www.countrybooksdirect.com
using our bank-approved, secure charging method.

"To anglers, photographs of themselves with the fish caught are open books. There's the story of it all."
Hook, Line & Thinker, p.193
Lough Currane, Ireland. 2003